Luciano Pavarotti

THE MYTH OF THE TENOR

Luciano Pavarotti

THE MYTH

OF THE

TENOR

by Jürgen Kesting

TRANSLATED BY

Susan H. Ray

Robson Books

First published in Great Britain in 1996 by Robson Books Ltd, Bolsover House, 5-6 Clipstone Street, London W1P 8LE

Originally published as *Luciano Pavarotti: Ein Essay über den Mythos der Tenorstimme*, copyright © 1991 by Econ Verlag Gmbh, Düsseldorf, Vienna and New York. English translation copyright © 1996 by Susan H Ray

British Library Cataloguing in Publication Data
A catalogue record for this title is available from the British Library

Designed by Virginia Evans

ISBN 1 86105 050 X

Printed and bound in Great Britain by Hartnolls Ltd, Bodmin, Cornwall

CONTENTS

Contents

PREFACE

In opera, as with any other performing art, to be in great demand and to command high fees you must be good, of course, but you must also be famous. They are two different things. The first thing always happens well before the second. Occasionally the second, fame, never happens for good talents. (And very rarely it happens without talent.) Sometimes, with good voices, fame is so slow to arrive that by the time the artist becomes widely known, he or she is no longer good, or not as good as they were. I think this was a little true with the great Maria Callas.

LUCIANO PAVAROTTI, "Making a Name," in
Pavarotti: My Own Story

*T*he baritone Victor Maurel, who sang the role of Iago in the premiere performance of Verdi's *Otello* and later the title role in *Falstaff* as well, used to say of Francesco Tamagno's singing, "C'est la voix unique du monde." These words expressed an artist's admiration for a tenor who, to quote one critic, "hurled" his high notes "through the hall with the force of an eight-inch mortar." When Giacomo

Puccini heard the young Enrico Caruso, he cried out in wonder, "Who sent you? God?"

Stories like these perpetuate the aura surrounding a being that doesn't seem to be of this world, but rather is a world unto itself: the tenor. The myth of the tenor has clung to Caruso for the past seventy years. The dust jacket of a book published on the twenty-fifth anniversary of Luciano Pavarotti's initial stage appearance repeated what had already been said about Benjamino Gigli, Mario Lanza, and Mario del Monaco: "Not since the era of Enrico Caruso has an opera star amassed as wide and admiring an audience—from opera aficionados to the general public—as . . ."[1] The names were interchangeable and will remain so, for this is the nature of myth.

The book just cited about today's heir to the myth is called *Grandissimo Pavarotti*. Hyperbole? Dust jackets tend to praise; titles or headlines tend to exaggerate. This title doesn't exaggerate and the dust jacket doesn't lie. When it comes to Luciano Pavarotti, overstatement is impossible: he is the very incarnation of hype.

Pavarotti is more than a singer, he's a Tenor, Inc. and Ltd., with a singer on as silent partner. This man is no longer a singing subject, but a voice, *the* voice. This omnipresent voice has transformed into modern "hits" whatever songs and arias hadn't already carved a niche for themselves on the popular music scene. "Nessun dorma" from Giacomo Puccini's *Turandot* became the victory march of the World Cup soccer team and took its place among the top titles on the charts. One wonders: An opera aria? Is it possible? The answer is yes. Topping the charts may still be a rarity for operatic arias, but not so their presence as the dinner music blaring out of stereo speakers in the local Ristorante Italiano or the neighborhood pizza parlor.

This voice has long since ceased to be synonomous with the voice of music. It has become entertainment. Pavarotti himself is no longer a singer, but the subject as well as the object of that entertainment, that gigantic industry whose sole purpose is to produce human happiness. He plays his role as subject with consummate skill, once in a while in an opera house but more frequently at expensive galas in less than elegant surroundings, on television, in shows, in clubs. Opera here, soap opera there—who can tell the difference anymore?

His appearances outside the opera house, so he claims, are meant to attract a new audience for this type of music. In fact, commercialism is what it's all about: opera, television, and Pavarotti himself. When he sings, he does more than sing: his smile transforms itself into a promo for his singing, for Pavarotti the product, diversified as CD and hoopla for brand-name cordials, concert tickets, videos, books, his own paintings. He even smiles for fur coats and credit cards.

Pavarotti has left far behind the old romantic role of the "artist as hero," to quote Wilfrid Mellers, the author of *Music and Society*. Many know him in the role of freak or monster—whatever the media happen to need at the moment. None of this is lost on Pavarotti: he knows he has to play different and mutually exclusive roles, all the while promoting his own identity as well. He has to be serious and silly, singer and clown, artist and tradesman. Who knows whether his following, which has increasingly come to resemble a cult of fanatics, actually hears him or merely goes along for the ride? Pavarotti is no longer famous because of the quality of his singing, but simply because he is so incredibly famous.

This book is a study of fame and an examination of the "Myth of the Tenor." As such it presents both historical analysis and critical assessment. Its purpose is not a hypocritical one: it does not aim to denigrate marketing techniques while simultaneously depending on them for its own promotion. Rather, its purpose is to go on record as objecting to the inconstancy of reception that capitulates in the face of fame, that considers discriminating critical appraisal as arrogant or elitist and accepts as the substance of art the synthetic and the simulated.

This book concentrates on the tenor voice and the voice of a tenor whose stage performances are limited to works composed between 1830 and 1930. It is not about a *voice of music* such as that of Nicolai Gedda, for instance, who placed his talents in the service of three centuries of this particular art form. It's about one voice that has managed to transform itself by modern means of mass communication and promotional hype into becoming "the unique voice in all the world."

PREFACE TO THE
ENGLISH-LANGUAGE EDITION

*T*his book was written immediately on the heels of a monograph on Maria Callas and while its author was still under the spell of the unique aesthetic challenge a female vocalist can present not only during her lifetime but for years afterward as well. Luchino Visconti said that "she did for opera what Verdi did for opera." An exaggeration, perhaps. But then, none less than Richard Wagner once wrote to Liszt that "the works of our poets and composers are mere desire," whereas the performance "is skill: that is the art."

Several of the Pavarotti concerts and performances that I attended in Dortmund, Berlin, and Hamburg as well as in New York were reminiscent of the Circus Maximus, the Berlin Sportpalast, or Caesar's Palace. Luciano Pavarotti caught my interest not only as a singer but because, as a living legend, he was a source of provocation as well. What I found particularly irritating was the glory and fame that had long since divorced itself from the singer, as unfortunately it had also done in the case of Maria Callas thirty years earlier. His name had come to represent a mythic commodity or even a household word, behind which the singer himself as well as the special quality of his art had disappeared.

{ x i }

The fact that prices rise for a capacity crowd actually contradicts the usual practices of the marketplace. But when the public is hoodwinked by the commodity hype and no longer recognizes how cheap, how banal, how trivial the special offers are, this only confirms what marketing sophisticates have always known: it's easier to sell people an expensive item than a cheap one.

Gala performances of world stars in the autumn of their career—whether it be Montserrat Caballé or José Carreras, Plácido Domingo or Luciano Pavarotti—are approaching epidemic proportions, but to raise a culturally critical hue and cry that such events represent little more than an overstimulation of the greed glands or, in the case of the audience, of a narcissistic lover, doesn't promise much improvement. Even so, one feels compelled to contradict the capitalist justification that the singers themselves studiously and repeatedly cite, namely, that galas in a luxurious circus atmosphere serve to attract a new and youthful audience to opera. The truth of the matter is that the star cult has managed to keep the public *away* from opera, at least in Europe, as long as the so-called superstars are not gracing the bill. These singers are selling only themselves—at prices in the neighborhood of five hundred dollars a ticket.

Over the past ten years Luciano Pavarotti and many others in his wake have represented opera in a highly dubious form—and themselves as well. In so doing Pavarotti has conceivably served many young singers as a bad example. At a time when the opera scene is floundering in a deep economic crisis, huge profits are being raked in through capacity sell-outs of aesthetic remainders. Luciano Pavarotti is world famous, but even if the talents that have made him so are by no means mere echoes of *tempi passati*, he is hardly in a position to display them when he routinely and smilingly repeats the same arias and songs at every opportunity.

One single deviation from the score in a *Don Carlo* performance or a few botched high C's—as in the Met's twenty-fifth-anniversary performance of *La Fille du Régiment*—are all it takes to make headlines in the tabloids, but this very fact is illustrative of nothing more than the revenge of the media cynics: in other words, the negative exploitation of his fame. It would have been a sensation indeed if a sixty-year-old had been able to outdo his younger self! The truly remarkable fact that, after thirty-five years on the stage, Pavarotti (like the constantly cited singers of the Golden Age between 1890 and 1910) still possesses a healthy, intact, virile voice, and can still sing with a delicately held legato, with eloquent diction, and with his own special timbre—all of this is left to the connoisseurs alone to discern and appreciate.

For this English edition, several passages that deal with Pavarotti's most recently released recordings have been added to bring the third chapter up to date.

Fame

Midcult *has the essential qualities of masscult but*

decently covers them with a cultural figleaf. It pretends

to respect the standards of high culture while in fact

it waters them down and vulgarizes them.

DWIGHT MCDONALD
"Masscult and Midcult"

VOX POPULI

*And then the already hefty Luciano Pavarotti emerged
from the background: Luciano Pavarotti, who, despite his
diet, still looks the way fettucine and rigatoni taste; but
now, with the voice that ranks as the crown jewel of the
guild he spits out the old familiar warhorses into the cultural scene of the summer stage: "Ridi Pagliaccio!," "E
lucevan le stelle," "Martha, Martha, du entschwandest."
The whole audience is turned on.*

KLAUS UMBACH, "Opera Bigwigs: Luciano
Pavarotti," in *Geldscheinsonate*[1]

*The objections to such performances are as old as they are
familiar: a motley program featuring mostly popular selections, chosen primarily to enhance the reputation of the
precious warbler . . . and not every superstar actually delivers in live performance what the PR hype promises. But
the "Evening of Songs and Arias" that Luciano Pavarotti
recently sang in the Alte Oper in Frankfurt proved to be an
accomplished demonstration of vocal quality and singing
technique even for the skeptic. . . . All the more impressive
was the fine nuance of Pavarotti's interpretations during
this performance, for there was truly much to admire. To*

begin with: a striking linearity and leanness of singing almost unexpected in its degree of virtuosity.

GERHARD R. KOCH, "The Colossal Tenor, or Concert in Costume," *Frankfurter Allgemeine Zeitung*, February 5, 1985

The scene: one evening in Berlin's National Opera House toward the end of February 1988. On the program is Gaetano Donizetti's *L'Elisir d'Amore*, a pretty piece containing a black pearl of melody, but not much more than the half flask of chianti the quack doctor sells to a naive peasant lad. Twenty or thirty years ago veteran ensemble groups would have considered this work a filler at best.

Yet Berlin's music lovers—in today's jargon, music *fans*—have been besieging the box office for days, as if *Otello* or *Tristan* were on the program. Hundreds upon hundreds revel in their anticipation, imagining how he will sing of the furtive tear that slipped from her eye, how they will applaud, and how he just might be induced to sing the ballad a second time. Yes, and then the record will be broken, there will surely be more than the one hundred–plus curtain calls with which the Spaniard's fans rewarded their idol only a few weeks before.

The fact that the hundred members of the Philharmonic reel off the overture with the brio of one of the better health resort orchestras wouldn't make any difference even if it were noticed. For there, onstage, the sun is rising—*he* appears. He is really there in all his mighty bulk, flashing his most charming smile and singing his brief opening song, "Quanto è bella, quanto è cara." Everyone in the audience hears and feels only "Quanto è bello, quanto è caro"—because he and only he is on the program: Luciano. Lucianissimo. *Tenorissimo.*

The air of high spirits isn't compromised in the least by the delivery of "Quanto è cara" with sunshine in the smile but no warmth in the voice. Very few notice that the wonderful, although hardly young Rolando Panerai still sings with the glorious sound and finesse of the *buffo* style. Nor does anyone complain about the person playing Belcore, whose ability to charge now lies only in the raw remnants of his voice. For whatever reasons, the star of the evening wanted him, and, after all, the star is what it's all about—the star alone, who mimics the clownish bear and spreads joy wherever he goes.

The moment everyone has been waiting for finally arrives: the five minutes that provoke the furtive tear: "Una furtive lagrima." He sings this graceful, elegaic *larghetto* capably and well—sings it with his impeccable diction, renders the long slurs with a taut phrasing, and lends the tender gestures eloquent expression. Yet the attack on the initial note, this emphasis on "una" in the shift from the chest to the head register, sounds a little dull, a little passive, even *piano*, but certainly not dolce. The crescendo leading into the twelfth bar is very demanding; it requires not only vocal but emotional and sensual exultation as well in the expressive "m'ama." Pavarotti's rendition sounds muffled, lacking the vocal projection that distinguishes the Caruso recording. He reproduces the ornate and blissful sigh with precision and confidence, but his *gruppeto* on "lo vedo" has nothing to offer by way of musical sweetness. Finally the cadenza, this coloratura sequence, swelling in four groups of sixteenth notes up to the high A. But haven't we heard this sung before with more energy and more elegance, with a more precise definition of the individual notes in the chain? And the final phrase, this achingly passionate sigh on "d'amore"—where is the bittersweet intonation of a Tito Schipa, a Ferruccio Tagliavini, where the all-consuming flaming passion of a Caruso, where that *morbidezza* capable of soothing a soul in purgatory?

The cheers ring out as loud and last as long in the opera house as they will in the op-ed pages of the next day's reviews: it's "neverending." At least that's what the Berlin papers will report. And there he is, standing like a statue of himself, with a blissful smile, outstretched arms, and bowed head in a deluge of applause. He nods to the conductor and delights the audience with a *da capo*. Delirium in the house, reacting more to a love potion than to a human voice. The audience, just waiting to be transported, hails him with wild acclaim bordering on the frenzied; all in all the cheering commands 115 or 117 bows—the number will vary and be inflated all the way up to 165 (in the *Spiegel* yet, that staid magazine of news and commentary!). In any case, it is a new record; the Spaniard has been outdone, and the VIPs in the Hotel Steigenberger will have to wait almost two full hours before the Big P finally strides into the banquet hall, replete with stage beard and makeup, draped in a colorful robe the size of a bedspread. The spotlights glare and now this, now that young lady clings to his neck; finally, long after midnight, he manages to slip into a smaller room and sit around a table with his sponsors. That's how beautiful opera can be when Pavarotti is there, even though it was actually an operatic evening featuring a work that, had he not appeared in it, would have aroused little more than a disdainful shrug of the shoulders.

Another evening one year later, this time in the Westphalian Hall in Dortmund. The atmosphere resembles that preceding a race, circensian games, or the German pop-music competition. To lift a phrase from Thomas Mann, the level of the audience is "humanely democratic." The overture from Donizetti's *Don Pasquale*, a curtain raiser à la summer spa concerts, builds up to a singular appearance: curious and fascinating at the same time, this heavyset man takes the stage with an agile swagger and, moving front and center, spreads his arms, embraces the crowd, throws his head back, and casts a smile that penetrates the darkest recesses of the back rows. His teeth sparkle like the stars in the aria from *Tosca*, while his left arm sports a small and fluttering badge. This is the long-awaited moment: Pavarotti singing the darlings of the opera, those arias that have been repeatedly savored by thousands of vocal cords and have long since carved a place for themselves within the ranks of popular tunes. He finishes up with musical postcards from the bay and back alleys of Naples.

Curious and fascinating also is the effect his voice has on the audience: it emerges from the mighty body and, amplified by microphone, literally fills the cavernous hall. This is not to say that the electronic amplification is in any way obtrusive or that it makes one's eardrums pound. The remarkable thing is how lean and tender it sounds, how, despite its consistent audibility, the voice seems to free itself from its physical origin and dissipate in air. The effect is close to that produced by Thomas Mann's ancient phonograph in *The Magic Mountain*: the tone seems somehow remote and reduced, rather like an object seen through an inverted spyglass. Connoisseurs might notice how smooth and accomplished the singer's rendition of Edgardo's final scene in *Lucia di Lammermoor* is, but there is little trace of the musical magnificence of a tenor voice, of high notes that strife the listener's ear like a missile, of the tremulous spell of ecstatic tonal projection.

Even the audience reaction has its own all-too-familiar ring to it, but one wonders what is actually being celebrated here. Are the crowds applauding him, or are they simply pleased by their good fortune in being part of an evening's cultural life whose tickets cost up to two hundred dollars each, in participating in an event that was simply going to be, had to be, fantastic, that could be nothing less than grandiose? Are they cheering because that's the only proper way to hail such an event? Are they cheering because they've just witnessed the phantom of the opera, a singer who, to quote *Time* magazine, "has hit the opera world with such seismic force" as "no other tenor in modern times"?[2] Or are they simply compelled to cheer because he's so enormously *simpatico*, not despite but *because* of his smiling, beaming corpulence?

Another evening, this time in New York's Metropolitan Opera House, February 1990. Verdi's *Rigoletto* is on the program, produced like a C movie without any noticeable direction of the characters. The members of the choral ensemble move about in the court scene like a bumbling village choir. The first brusque passages of dialogue, sung with a fine *parlando*, already make Pavarotti the focus of attention: it's not his physical presence that fascinates but his vocal precision, his plastic, crystalline diction. The aria "Questa o quella" proves as difficult for him as it in fact is; he simply doesn't have the verve to give the *acuti* their striking accents. In order to collect himself, he leaves a few notes out just before the brief concluding cadenza.

No reaction from the audience. In fact, during the following *duettino* between the Duke and the Countess Ceprano ("Partite, crudele"), they either aren't listening or don't have a clue as to what's going on. This is the scene in which the cynical libertine sets to work, seducing one of the ladies of the court with his honey-coated phrases—and Pavarotti sings these *passaggio* phrases in a truly high musical fashion, softly and yet full-bodied. Again no reaction on the part of the audience. In his next big scene, during the overlapping conclusion to the duet with Gilda ("Addìo, addìo speranza ed anima!"), what's in store for him is a huge leap all the way up to D flat. It's an optional note for the tenor; he doesn't have to sing it, but he has done so before with gusto and radiance, especially on his recordings. Isn't this what his fans, until now not terribly alert, are hoping to hear?

One would presume that a singer like Pavarotti knows exactly when his voice is supple enough to reach the top notes. He throws his head back and advances to front stage—and in New York, yet. But what does he do? While still lingering over "Addìo" he takes the hand of his Gilda and raises it to his lips in such a way as to form a funnel with his own hands. The note trumpets through this mouthpiece and emerges a little diffuse, a little dull. A vocalist's conjuring trick. The audience hardly notices, or if it does, it doesn't react.

The cut in the second act doesn't seem to attract any attention, either. Pavarotti sings the great aria "Ella mi fu rapita—Parmi veder le lagrime," again with considerable effort in the soft tones of the *passaggio* region. But he omits entirely the cabaletta "Possente amor" following the concluding chorus of "Duca, duca"; he has always sung this on his recordings as well as on film, and has always crowned it with an endless high D. Tonight it's evident to all that he's no longer up to such a tour de force. "Why should I expose myself to such a risk," he once asked a journalist, "when I know I'm no longer in shape?"

The obligatory cheers naturally follow the canzone "La donna è mobile," but the jolt on the Richter scale doesn't indicate an earthquake.

It's the evening after the final game of the World Cup soccer match. A summit meeting has been announced. Two orchestras and three tenors, united under the baton of Zubin Mehta, are to give a gala performance in the Baths of Caracalla: Pavarotti along with the two Spaniards Plácido Domingo and José Carreras. Does any singer have a more inveterate worst enemy than a camera that looks him in the eye and reveals his every strain, including the emergence of pencil-thick veins along the neck, the tensing of muscles, the backward thrusts of the head accompanying the A's, the B flats, or the B's? (The C didn't even appear on the program.) Pavarotti is the only one not to show (almost) any sign of such strain. His mouth forms a beautiful, round O, his teeth sparkle, his eyes laugh, his tongue lies flat in his mouth and doesn't inhibit his breathing. In short, he shows his younger colleagues a thing or two.

A performer-friendly appraisal of the evening would call it a sophisticated artistic lark; an objective evaluation would describe it as a perfectly produced piece of musical marketing rather like a shift from bel canto to bel conto, to borrow a pun from Klaus Umbach.³ It goes without saying that the event was visually as well as acoustically recorded and came out on video, CD, phonograph records, and music cassettes. Naturally it sold enough copies to turn the record to gold, just like everything else that's touched by "opera's golden tenor,"⁴ this Midas of the vocal chords. One of his albums, *Tutti Pavarotti,* which features a selection from his extensive discography, sold more than a million copies alone. That's easily double if not triple what even established singers earn from their recital recordings.

Maria Callas was the only postwar celebrity who managed to attract as much attention to herself as does the man from Modena, even though not exactly in her role as singer. Like her, he too is more than a singer—or better said, a singer and then some. He's a mass phenomenon that has long since ceased to be heard and measured against objective musical or aesthetic criteria. His fame has absorbed all the elements of the tenor myth and has metamorphosed into an internationally recognized trademark.

Isn't there something fishy about this? Can that really be the reward of honest artistic work? Or has this singer, who earns close to a quarter million dollars an evening for his guest appearances in mass arenas and luxury hotels, been transformed into an entertainer or even an enterprise, "Pavarotti, Inc.," as the magazines that played such a contributing role in his buildup so cynically write today? What happened to Pavarotti the opera singer? Or has opera itself

become nothing more than a quarry for presumably sophisticated highbrow hits—at least the opera industry as we
know it, that of the stars and the festivals? Has he become
the symbolic figure for this metamorphosis, or for what
accountants call "turnover"?

OF KINGS AND POTENTATES

*The absence of kings and princes seems also to have fostered
a craving for surrogate royalty; in any event, the cult of
personality, dragging high culture downward, has for over
a century more dramatically articulated the musical scene
here [in the United States] than abroad. The technological
machinery of twentieth-century midcult, finally, is first and
foremost American machinery impacting on marketing,
scale, emotional pitch, and personal style.*

JOSEPH HOROWITZ, *Understanding Toscanini*

$\mathcal{W}$e are living in the age of fame and celebrity. As the
historian Daniel Boorstin once said, a celebrity is "a
person who is well known for his well-knownness."[1] Twenty
years ago such a celebrity would still have been called a "star,"
ten years ago he had to be a "superstar," and today, as
happens with all hyperbole, you only begin to count once
you're a "megastar." The standard for this designation lies
solely and squarely in the magic of the big number: the size
of the audience, the number of copies sold, the amount of

the agent's fee—as if they weren't also indicators of the fad quotient—and, above all, the number of zeros on the paycheck.

This phenomenon can only be explained by the psychosomatics of the spirit of the age—or should I say the age of spirits?—namely, as a narcissistic object choice. The meteoric rise of the star/superstar/megastar doesn't depend on personal talent; its emergence depends solely on the degree to which what is promoted as the star's drawing power fulfills the expectations of its public, which, in turn, is hardly able to make a discriminating critical judgment regarding even the qualities of a competent artisan, let alone a master. The genius thus propagated by marketing techniques and public relations is forced, as it were, to promote his artistic self as a secularized icon, rather like Herbert von Karajan, whom posters and record albums portrayed as absorbed in himself and his music. Even so, people still want to know what kind of person the great artist is, what his hobbies are and what his sexual preferences, where and how he lives, what make of car he drives, what discos he frequents and where he spends his leisure time. In short, in keeping with "the man is the message" mentality, the artist has to transform himself into a talk show personality or, since the "exchange mentality"[2] stops at nothing and no one, he has to become at one and the same time a product and its own personalized promotion.

In his *Critique of Cynical Reason*, Peter Sloterdijk takes exception to Georg Simmel's *Philosophy of Money*. Sloterdijk maintains that "values" don't fall under the rubric of products that can be bought for money. Simmel says, "The more money becomes the sole center of interests, the more we see honor and conviction, talent and virtue, beauty and the health of the soul mobilized on its behalf, all the more will a mocking and frivolous mood arise regarding these higher goods of life, which are offered for sale for the same kind of value (*Wertquale*) as goods on the weekly market." Sloterdijk carries this idea over to modern times and comes to a different conclusion: "Only in a situation of universal seduction (in which, moreover, those who were seduced have long regarded the word 'corruption' as morally overstrained) can Simmel's 'frivolous mood' regarding the higher goods of life (from now on, so-called higher goods of life) become a cultural climate."[3]

The magical transformation of an artist into a king, of a man into a message, and of the talents he possesses into exchange rates, has a name: Luciano Pavarotti. The name itself conjures up divine/demonic images: in the mid-1970s, Pavarotti sang the role of Arturo in Vincenzo Bellini's *I Puritani* at the Metropolitan Opera in New York (a role, incidentally, made famous by Giovanni Battista Rubini). In response, *Newsweek* introduced "The Great Pavarotti" in an article spiced with enough anecdotes for a Hollywood script. Ever since then he has been described and idolized by an exaggerated hype ever intent upon outdoing itself. He's been dubbed "Big P," "Opera's Golden Tenor," "Lucianissimo," the "King of High C's," "Grandissimo Pavarotti," and, with the frivolity of sexual innuendo, "Deep Throat," or else simply "the King."[4]

The emergence of an artist from the protected or restricted domain of so-called serious music and his buildup to the rank of star/superstar/megastar have never been undertaken more systematically or more successfully than in the case of Pavarotti. True, he puts in what athletes would call "home games" at New York's Metropolitan Opera and "away games" in Paris, Vienna, and Berlin, as well as in this or that provincial theater that now and again can grant him and his audience the honor. But his "championship games" all take place in sports arenas and other such enormous outdoor stadia. His status as a television star guarantees a mass audience, for it is much more than merely that of an opera singer. It encompasses his popularity and fame as well as his disarming smile, which is not only a smile but the celebrated radiance of "O sole mio."

This endearing smile, this living postcard depicting the charm of Italian warmth, also beams for American Express credit cards—a fact that has received harsh comment from several critics who refuse to accept the lax ethical standards it betrays. When questioned by a reporter for *People* magazine, Pavarotti said, "There are things that will bring this little world of opera to a larger audience, and I don't care how we do it. We have to go to the people, and if someone doesn't understand, it is too bad."[5] To another fan-oriented magazine, *Ovation*, he has said, "If it would fill a 10,000-seat theater every night for opera, I would sell margarine on TV—and be proud of it."[6] Such an attitude is difficult to counter because of its deliberate "democratic" flavor. It fits the cliché of the artist lending his weight where it counts, easing the unsophisticated public of its awe for the "swells" by renouncing the supposedly elitist character of opera.

Herbert Breslin, Pavarotti's longtime manager, hits the nail on the head when he writes on "managing Pavarotti" in his section of the singer's autobiography: "I suppose it's an unhappy commentary on our culture, but those television commercials he did for the American Express cards familiarized more people with Luciano than eighteen years of superb singing in the world's opera houses. So these stints are useful for his recognizability."[7] Of course, this statement distorts the image of the star to a total resemblance of the facts, to borrow a pun from Ernst Bloch. Pavarotti has to be recognizable to the masses, and he can become so only by being a permanent interviewee of *Playboy, People, Brigitte, Il Giorno*—*e tutti quanti.* He's even played tennis with John McEnroe for as long as it took to "serve, return, smile, and click." "Ehi, Luciano: son qua! Luciano qua, Luciano là, Luciano su, Luciano giù. Pronto, prontissimo. Son come il fulmine. Sono il factotum . . ." But he's not the factotum of the city, he's the factotum of the industry as a whole: he is its universal metaphor.

In his book *The Art of Singing*, William James Henderson, whose sharp, even biting remarks would expose any critic who made them today to the risk of a civil suit, granted the singer carte blanche to "make hay while the sun shines."[8] And who in the history of singing hasn't been guided by this maxim? Several of the most successful castrati sang themselves into possession of huge landed estates. Adelina Patti earned as much in one evening as the president of the United States earns in a year and, when reproachfully confronted with this fact, is said to have replied, "Let him sing."

Be that as it may, even a Caruso, the first "plebian tenor"—he was a singer of the common folk, and the myth surrounding him is based on the typically American rise-to-fame success story—received fees for his late solo stints in South America that, when calculated at today's rates, were the equivalent of sums in the six-figure range, and he left an estate, again in terms of today's buying power, worth well over fifty million dollars.[9]

Envy comes in many guises, even the critical. As Rolv Heuer demonstrated in his captivating book *Genius and Wealth*, there is such a thing as a curious "physiology of the purse," and an even more curious psychology of historians, biographers, and reviewers (into whose ranks, according to Hans Magnus Enzensberger, even the once serious critics have shriveled and shrunk).[10] Heuer writes, "The same spirit that makes words and creates values also fills wallets and swells bank accounts. People are unwilling to excuse this. Several centuries of historical documentation have trained us to look upon the great works of the great minds as gifts to mankind. . . . The idea that the genius takes money for his talent strikes us as obscene. But what else should he take for it? The world's gratitude doesn't fill a stomach. Why shouldn't posthumous fame in this world justify an advance during the artist's lifetime? Every brain is connected to a gut. . . . Talent has a sweet scent, but money stinks. The adoration accorded the genius helps alleviate the stench of lucre; it's a proven deodorant. We're not talking about what belongs to the genius. That's unseemly, it just isn't done. To the genius belongs a place in our hearts."[11]

The last thing I as critic want to do here is elevate a singer to the ranks of genius; what I do want to do is expose the psychology behind a critique that is being deliberately propagated by the media, whose owners surely come off no less handsomely with what Peter Sloterdijk calls information cynicism than does an established musician.[12] Criticism of unusually financially successful musicians, of whom there are surely fewer than there are successful merchants and business tycoons, rests on the insinuation that money does indeed stink. And this type of criticism is marked by a sensational style. According to Sloterdijk, "the packaging lies with its sensationalizing style by continually restoring a long since superseded, morally primitive frame of reference in order to be able to present the sensations as something that falls outside these coordinates." One might add that this is the case when it presents the monstrous idea that a first-class singer should pocket ten or twenty thousand dollars an evening. It hardly ever occurs to one of the media moralists that top sports stars are occasionally paid ten times that amount for one tournament title.[13]

Add to that the fact that successful artists are by no means only snug bugs in the culture rug; they are also courted by politicians and businessmen. The opera houses, the theaters, the concert halls may owe their origin to a bygone bourgeois pride in culture, but today they are governmentally subsidized under such catchwords as local color, tourism, or pork-barrel financing. This is because they are no longer indirect economic factors or even window dressing for that which big business calls corporate identity and which VIPs visiting the cultural fairs glorify with the elevated and edifying maxim "Man does not live by bread alone."

The fact remains, strange and anachronistic, that precisely those people who most willingly "climb into bed with mercenary fame" (Klaus Umbach) or, as managers, act as pimps to the stars, use their Sunday sermons and ethical righteousness to transfigure the moral, aesthetic, or socially hygienic significance of culture—as if this were not an aestheticized negative image of a market condition that has universalized the exchange principle.

The star/superstar/megastar Pavarotti plays only one part in this game. An ideal billboard, he is the one who lends the most beautiful voice to this strange symphony.

AN IRRESISTIBLE RISE

*From the start, I never doubted Luciano would one day be
a very great tenor. It wasn't only the voice, it was his
approach to the work—he was dedicated, mature, alert. He
wasn't dabbling, he was totally serious about
perfecting his voice.*

ARRIGO POLA, "Teaching Pavarotti,"
in *Pavarotti: My Own Story*

$\mathcal{P}$ avarotti set out on a route not unlike that pursued by
many before him: five years of training (between 1955
and 1960), followed by ten years of a completely normal
career and another six or seven years devoted to the climb to
fame. What happened in those ten years or so, if it wasn't, as
it so often is, a *descent* into stardom? Nothing unusual or even
sensational marked the early years. The son of Fernando
Pavarotti, a baker who also happened to be gifted with an
unusual singing voice but was plagued by stage fright, Luciano finished school, worked for a short time as a teacher,
and at the age of twenty began his studies under Arrigo Pola,

a tenor who had not made a significant career for himself but who was an excellent teacher. Pavarotti's first impressions of what a tenor voice sounded like and how it made music came from recordings of the great singers of his day: Enrico Caruso, Aureliano Pertile, Benjamino Gigli, Tito Schipa, Mario del Monaco, and Giuseppe di Stefano.[1]

Pola apparently adhered to the old tried-and-true rules and maxims. He worked with his student on scales and the proper articulation of notes and vowels, the sine qua non for mechanically clean singing—eternalized in a perhaps apocryphal but still splendid anecdote about the lessons the castrato Gaetano Caffarelli (1703–83) received from the singer and composer Nicola Porpora (1686–1766). The latter is said to have written out a single sheet of technical exercises based on vowel sounds for his student and required him to sing them every day. After six endless and fatiguing years, he is said to have dismissed Caffarelli with the words "I have nothing further to teach you—you are the greatest singer in the world."[2]

Unlike many who begin their training with arias and songs, Pavarotti did not start by studying songs, but rather by studying singing, as strange as that might seem. Instead of beginning with expression and interpretation, this approach ends with them—and its prerequisite is the total control of technique. Control over scales, ornaments, and trills is to be demanded as much of the singer as of every other musician. However seductive may be the sensual charm that engenders the cult surrounding the so-called beautiful or golden voice, it has nothing to do with the art of singing. In his book on Pavarotti, Martin Mayer justifiably points out that the pianist Rudolf Serkin—by no means an advocate for empty virtuosity—reintroduced the study of solfeggio (i.e., training the eye to read and the ear to recognize chromatic relationships as well as the usual scales) not only for singers, but for pianists and violinists as well, when he took up his post as director of the Curtis Institute of Music in Philadelphia.[3]

During his early studies under Pola, Pavarotti earned his living first as a teacher and then as an insurance agent. With melodramatic eloquence he later revealed that the rhetorical endurance exercises required to woo clients did harm to his singing voice. In 1957, when Arrigo Pola betook himself and his activities as singer and teacher to Japan, which was then the newly emergent and rapidly expanding market for classical music, Pavarotti turned to Ettore Campogalliani in Mantua for further instruction. After three more years of study, during which, in his own words, he sang here and there with a "small, subtle, and interesting, mellow, sweet, and round voice,"[4] he quit his job at the insurance agency and concentrated solely on his singing. He was rewarded in the spring of 1961 when he won a competition, the Peri Prize, in Piacenza, whose jury, by the way, was headed by Mafalda Favero. This recognition enabled him to make his debut as Rodolfo in Puccini's *La Bohème* under the direction of

Francesco Molinari-Pradelli in the provincial capital of Reggio nell'Emilia. Molinari-Pradelli immediately informed the young tenor that the "dictatorship of the baton," so bemoaned by Verdi but generally accepted since Toscanini, was still in force. Molinari-Pradelli ("The best arm I have ever seen," according to Pavarotti) was later to conduct at Pavarotti's debuts in Milan's Scala, New York's Met, and in Verona's Arena.

What wouldn't we give to hear how the young Enrico Caruso or Maria Callas sounded in their debuts? As it happens, excerpts from "Il Debutto di Pavarotti" are available on a recording with a thoroughly acceptable sound quality, because the writer Vladimir Nabokov had commissioned a friend to make a live tape of the debut of his son Dmitri, who sang the part of Colline. In spite of a few insecurities, understandable in the case of a beginner, Pavarotti gave more than a merely respectable performance. The pleasant memory of this happy evening may be behind his description of the acoustics of the Teatro Municipale with its thousand seats as being the best he has ever known. What is certain is that nothing better could have happened to a young lyric tenor than to begin in a small house where there was no need to project. The recording also shows that he accentuated several of the interjections in the quasi-dialogue scenes of the first act perhaps a bit too forcefully and that he rendered the extremely difficult phrases of the aria starting with "Talor dal mio forziere" with too much volume. Put another way, and perhaps less critically, one could say that he didn't sing it here as leanly and delicately as he later did on the subtle recording under the direction of Herbert von Karajan. The pressure on the C at the end of the first act betrays the inner compulsion he must have felt to show what he could do. Nevertheless, the success encouraged him to marry his fiancée, Adua Veroni.

At the behest of an agent who immediately took him on, Pavarotti spent the following spring studying four different parts: the Duke in *Rigoletto*, Edgardo in *Lucia di Lammermoor*, Alfredo in *La Traviata*, and Pinkerton in *Madama Butterfly*. These were the only parts he was to sing during his first two seasons, the plan being that they would establish a certain degree of local recognition. On March 15, 1962, he sang the first of four performances as the Duke in *Rigoletto* in Palermo under the direction of Tullio Serafin, who, at close to eighty-four, was much too old to act as career maker, as he had once done for Rosa Ponselle and Maria Callas. Pavarotti told me how he had once sung an ostentatious cadenza during one of the early rehearsals and had been reprimanded by Serafin for having done so. But then in the dress rehearsal he was suddenly supposed to sing this cadenza after all, and Serafin stunned the singer as well as the members of the orchestra with the words "This cadenza is absolutely right for the young man." Later he told the puzzled tenor, "You know, my son, your applause is my applause as well."

Like so many singers of our times, and this applies to the most talented as well, Pavarotti never got the chance to develop his technique in an established company, as had been the norm before the 1950s. He made guest appearances wherever he could: following the *Rigoletto* performance in Palermo he sang in Forlì, Bari, Rovigo, Bologna, and Piacenza, and then, starting on January 18, 1963, in Utrecht, the Hague, and Rotterdam. On February 24 he debuted as Rodolfo at the Vienna State Opera, where he also sang the Duke a short time later ("vocal virtuosity, but no heart," wrote Karl Löbl at the time), and in September of the same year he finally came to the Royal Opera at Covent Garden. Once again he sang the role of the poet in Puccini's artist opera, substituting for the unreliable Giuseppe di Stefano. That he sang his next performances as the Duke, Rodolfo, and Alfredo in Ankara, Budapest, and Barcelona indicates that he was still looking to establish his career on the road, as it were—and that he was still far from being considered a star.

On the other hand, the twelve performances as Idamante in Mozart's *Idomeneo* that he sang in Glyndebourne in July 1964 were significant. They established his name in the English-speaking world (the artistic qualities will be discussed later) and also led to the all-important "Sutherland connection." May 1964 found him in London, where he sang Elvino next to Joan Sutherland's Amina in Bellini's *La Sonnambula*, after which he accompanied the diva on an Australian tour. On December 9, 1965, he debuted as the

Duke at La Scala; in the following three months he also sang Rodolfo and Teobaldo in Bellini's *I Capuleti e i Montecchi* in the same house. This proved to be a highly controversial production under the direction of Claudio Abbado, because the role of Romeo, which the composer had intended for a soprano, was sung by Giacomo Aragall. Despite the uncontested successes Pavarotti had behind him, Herbert von Karajan still preferred the experienced Carlo Bergonzi for soloist in Verdi's Requiem at a 1966 Scala star performance in Montreal. However, when the conductor performed the same piece to mark the hundredth anniversary of the birth and the tenth anniversary of the death of Arturo Toscanini at La Scala on January 16 and 18, 1967, it was Pavarotti who sang next to Leontyne Price, Fiorenza Cossotto, Shirley Verrett, and Nicolai Ghiaurov.

On June 24 of that year he sang the first of five performances of the comic opera *La Fille du Régiment* (in French) at Covent Garden, and the evening proved a momentous one. The role of Tonio, which he had to learn phonetically, lies in a very high tessitura, with no less than nine high C's in the aria "Pour mon âme—Ah, mes amis" alone. According to Martin Mayer, Pavarotti is said to have "thrown them off like rice at a wedding,"[5] a feat he repeated six years later at the New York Metropolitan Opera and at other performances in Boston, Cleveland, Atlanta, Memphis, New Orleans, Minneapolis, and Detroit. This tour de force is said to have established his reputation in the United States.

It certainly fits in well with the story of a career—what better confirmation of a tenor sensation than a salvo of C's? But Alan Jefferson's review in *Opera*, on the other hand, tells of a production that completely missed the mark both scenically and theatrically. The critic merely praised the exemplary singing of the diva, while of the tenor he wrote, "Luciano Pavarotti had the audience tense with excitement, then rapturous with applause over the successive high C's in the Act I aria; . . . the sound of these notes is, to me, more remarkable than beautiful."[6] Nevertheless, La Scala produced the work eighteen months later; this time Mirella Freni sang the role of Marie. Claudio Sartori's review, again in *Opera*, speaks ecstatically about this performance.[7]

Pavarotti made his American debut in the role of Rodolfo at the San Francisco Opera on November 11, 1967, with Mirella Freni singing Mimi. It was a unique guest appearance and was followed exactly one year later, in October and November 1968, by four performances of Donizetti's *Lucia di Lammermoor* with Margherita Rinaldi. Pavarotti was later to try out many of his new roles on the West Coast: Ricardo in *Un Ballo in Maschera*, Fernando in *La Favorita*, Rodolfo in *Luisa Miller*, Manrico in *Il Trovatore*, Calaf in *Turandot*, Enzo in *La Gioconda*, and Radames in *Aïda*, all simultaneously preparations for his appearances at the Met. There, however, he had less success in his debut as Rodolfo on November 23, 1968. He was so ill he had to break off the second performance after the second act. In 1969 he sang almost exclusively in Italy, primarily at La Scala (Rodolfo, Tonio, and Des Grieux in *Manon*), but five performances of Bellini's *I Puritani* in Bologna were significant. At the beginning of the next season (1969–70), he made another attempt to break into the American scene: he appeared in four performances respectively of *La Bohème* and *L'Elisir d'Amore* in San Francisco. After two guest appearances in Mexico City he sang in only twenty-four performances in Italy for the rest of the season, which is to say, from November 1969 to May 1970.

In October of that year he made a comeback singing with Renata Scotto in four performances of *Lucia di Lammermoor* and two of *La Traviata* with Joan Sutherland at the Met. The role of Edgardo is surely one of his best and most effective, and he sang it next to Joan Sutherland, Beverly Sills, Margherita Rinaldi, Virginia Zeani, Cristina Deutekom, Edda Moser, and Luciana Serra. On the other hand, he sings Alfredo well but doesn't like the part—*La Traviata* is simply a soprano's opera, and it's difficult to win the audience's heart in the role of the bourgeois mediocrity that Alfredo unquestionably is.

Hearts are more easily won by Nemorino in Donizetti's *L'Elisir d'Amore*, which Pavarotti sang on December 8, 1970, at the season opening of La Scala. Until then he had sung the part of the true-hearted peasant lad only in Australia during his tour with Sutherland, then twice in Modena in 1968, and four times in San Francisco in October 1969. He later carved out his own niche in the history of this piece by playing the part of the naive Nemorino with sophistication: he turned it into an ironic self-representation, a good-natured ridicule of the doltish tenor. These performances were followed, almost monotonously, by guest appearances as Edgardo-Rodolfo-the Duke just about everywhere: between March 10 and October 1971 the young star sang only two roles, Rodolfo and the Duke. After five performances of Verdi's *Un Ballo in Maschera* in San Francisco, starting on October 25 and continuing to the end of the 1971–72 season, all that came his way was Rodolfo, Edgardo, Tonio, and once, Arturo in *I Puritani* next to Beverly Sills.

In hindsight, the salvo of high C's in the fifteen performances of Donizetti's *La Fille du Régiment* in New York and in seven other American cities launched his career as an opera singer. Pavarotti admits as much: "I sang at the Metropolitan for a number of years before the New York audience at large became aware of my existence. It was not enough," he wrote in *My Own Story*, "to sing beautiful high C's in *Bohème* or *Lucia*. I had to sing *nine* high C's in a row in *The Daughter of the Regiment* before I won their attention."[8] Be that as it may, he advanced to top billing at the Met, where he sang in more than a dozen performances during the ten weeks between December 1, 1972, and February 10, 1973—again as Rodolfo, Edgardo, Tonio, the Duke, and Riccardo. By the middle of the 1970s he had expanded his repertoire only by the addition of Fernando in *La Fa-*

vorita and Rodolfo in *Luisa Miller*, without, however, exceeding his technical limits, even though the Verdi part was already causing some strain. If he hadn't taken these precautions, he would surely not have been able to preserve his voice, a sensitive instrument because of its translucence and subtle glaze, as long as he has. After one glance at the score, he had enough sense to say no when La Scala offered him the part of Arnoldo in *Guglielmo Tell*; those 456 G's, 93 A's, 54 B flats, 15 B's, 19 C's, and 2 C sharps that James Joyce once tallied up scared the pants off him.[9] It is regrettable, though, that he never sang one single Rossini role and rejected a Mozart role like that of Fernando, which Sir Georg Solti offered him at Covent Garden. Perhaps because it was not a starring role?

On the other hand, after Elvino in *La Sonnambula*, he did sing the role of Arturo in Bellini's *Puritani* next to Joan Sutherland, Sherrill Milnes, and the young James Morris under the direction of Richard Bonynge. As happened just about two decades earlier to Maria Callas, whom a cover story in *Time* transformed into the *diva furiosa* before her debut at the Met, the ten performances starting on February 25, 1976, turned a successful singer into a chimera: "The Great Pavarotti." *Newsweek* described an insatiable "Latin lover" and a true gargantuan with a weight that, according to the magazine, friends estimated at a flattering 350 pounds and enemies set at an exaggerated 400. It quoted his anxious confessions regarding the high range of his part, as if it were a dance on a tightrope with no safety net below, and spiced the story with all kinds of scurrilous anecdotes from the inexhaustible arsenal of legends that inform the history of the guild.

The references to his singing itself, however, remained vague and global. "*I Puritani* calls for a tenor who can sing at full strength almost continuously in the upper part of his register. Pavarotti is one of the very few tenors alive who can do that, but even he has transposed the role's highest notes, two D's and an impossible F above high C, down to a next-to-impossible C-sharp. 'It's like a non-stop high jump where the bar is always at world-record level,' he said."[10] This somewhat dramatic description says little more than that singing requires a high degree of athletic energy. It says nothing about the technical aspects of singing, particularly those concerning the production of sound; it fails to say that tenors in the first three or four decades of the nineteenth century always sang the high A *di petto*, that is, with the full sound of the chest voice; and it even fails to give an adequate technical or aesthetic analysis and represents singing as if tenors, like body builders, were simply showing off their muscles.

Newsweek featured this article in its March 15, 1976, issue; the reporter was thus able to quote from an interview that Richard Bonynge, the conductor of the performance, had given in *Opera News* on February 28. Particularly interesting are Bonynge's remarks about the tenor's voice and technique: "I would classify him as a strong lyric tenor," he said; "he has a voice that records very dramatically, and close up it sounds like a dramatic, but from the middle of the theater it sounds like a strong lyric. He can sing a beautiful *legato* line, and very lyrically. His high F in our recent *Puritani* recording is a *falsetto* that he just happens to have by nature; I think the nineteenth-century *falsetto* sound was more steely, more focused and better integrated into the rest of the voice. Luciano can sing well up to the high D-flat from the chest, but beyond that isn't possible for a voice of that size."[11]

Whether the "supercilious scorn"[12] with which some New York critics showered the production of *I Puritani* is justified or not is neither here nor there. Pavarotti himself has always said—and sufficiently proven—that artists are not as stupid as certain reviewers generally represent them to be, and they are also perfectly capable of self-criticism. It ought to be obvious that it's not enough for a singer to learn from a review that "the tenor was not in good voice." Who, if not the singer himself, is more aware of such things? By the same token, who can imagine how a singer feels to hear himself portrayed as a freak in the original meaning of the word? "Luciano Pavarotti tops the scales in brilliance, bulk and brio," announced the headline of *Time*'s cover story on September 24, 1979. The article continued: "At six feet and nearly 300 lbs., 'Big P.,' as the soprano Joan Sutherland calls him, is more than life-size, as is everything about him—his clarion high Cs, his fees of $8000 per night for an opera and $20,000 for a recital, his Rabelaisian zest for food and fun."[13]

Upon reading such reviews, most of us are left with the question, So what? Haven't we gotten used to this kind of hype? Hasn't public attention long since focused more on a celebrity's fame and less on the talent that made the artist famous in the first place? It's easy and accepted practice to criticize established artists for getting involved in the deceptive, evil game of harlotry that their climb to fame frequently is, and for them to complain only when they are accused of prostitution—only the question remains: By whom? Peter Sloterdijk described the contradiction this way: "Who is edifying, and who the edified? Cynicism goes hand in hand with a diffusion of the knowing subject, so that today's system slave can easily do with the right hand what the left hand would never allow. Colonizer during the day, colonized in the evening; by profession exploiter and bureaucrat, as a person of leisure exploited and bureaucratized; publicly a cynic, privately a sensitive guy . . . outwardly a realist, inwardly a hedonist. . . . This mish-mash is our moral status quo."[14]

The production of the Bellini opera can be considered a turning point in the singer's career. He was flying high in every sense of the word. Pavarotti's own feelings about the *Puritani* production was that it was the crown of his career: he had conquered a role not only exemplary and symbolic but surrounded by the aura of legend as well. Moreover, because there were no greater heights to conquer, not even in the technical realm, he also had to change his own image and that of the professional tenor as well. During the 1976–

77 season he sang the role of Manrico in *Il Trovatore* at the
Met for the first time, a role he had perfected in eight
performances in San Francisco the year before. In addition,
he sang Cavaradossi in seven performances of *Tosca* in Chicago and four in London. The only lyric role he sang during
this season, which tallied a grand total of only forty-three
operatic performances, was that of Nemorino in the Hamburg State Opera. He was in excellent form and dominated
the performance next to the splendid singing of Giuseppe
Taddei. There were a total of forty-seven performances in
the 1977–78 season, beginning once again with Nemorino (in
Chicago) and including a trial run of the role of Calaf in
Turandot next to Montserrat Caballé in San Francisco.
Pavarotti later described this part to a critic as a "dream role"
and qualified it in his response to the follow-up question as
a "nightmare." He dropped it forever after seven performances. At the Met that year he sang only eight times, six
as Fernando in Donizetti's *La Favorita* and twice as Nemorino, and followed this up by trying his voice at Manrico in
the Arena of Verona. The 1978–79 season saw only thirty-
eight performances, in twenty-one of which he sang the role
of the painter in *Tosca*, in another seven that of Rodolfo in
La Bohème under the direction of Carlos Kleiber at La Scala.
At the beginning of the 1979–80 season, he once again made
the role of Enzo in *La Gioconda* his own. In San Francisco
he sang a *spinto* role, which he repeated at the end of the
season in five performances in Verona. In between came

seven *Rigolettos* in Chicago; Munich was treated to five performances of *Un Ballo in Maschera*; there were fifteen performances at the Met as well as guest appearances as part of the Met Ensemble; eight performances of *Tosca* at La Scala; and, finally, another six Nemorinos back in the United States.

In the 1980s, Pavarotti had to adhere to a stricter diet during his operatic appearances than he did during his "do-re-mi-fat"15 cures so ballyhooed in the trade magazines. In 1980–81 he sang in twenty-three performances, followed by twenty-seven in the next season; in 1982–83 he could be seen and heard in forty-one operatic productions; this dropped to thirty-six in 1983–84, and in that same year he appeared in exactly sixteen productions. During all these years his repertoire grew by only three roles. November 12, 1981, found him in San Francisco, where he sang Radames in *Aïda* for the first time, and he soon repeated it in Berlin (March 1982), Chicago (September 1983), Vienna (April 1984), London (June 1984), Milan (December 1985), and finally in New York (March 1986). Under James Levine he prepared for the title role of Mozart's *Idomeneo* for the New York Metropolitan performance of that work in October 1982, and he sang this role under the same conductor in Salzburg in July and August of the following year. Finally, in November 1983 he sang the title role of Giuseppi Verdi's *Ernani* in New York, again under the baton of James Levine.

The number of his recitals and so-called gala performances increased in inverse proportion to the number of his
operatic appearances; to the same degree as his fame became
more established, the critical tone of his reviewers sharpened,
curiously as well as typically in the magazines that had previously greeted him with fanfares. One headline in *Time* of
November 30, 1981, read: "What Price Pavarotti Inc.?" The
subtitle announced: "In a new role, the one-man conglomerate sells singing short."[16] The reviewer Michael Walsh wrote
about the wearing out of the "sweet voice" that had made "its
owner the most affecting Rodolfo of his generation," about
the high notes that sounded sudden and strained, and about
the missed high B flat at the end of the romance, which had
been "belted out rough and ragged with a desperate *fortissimo.*" "One wonders why Pavarotti, 46, is risking his voice
and reputation on parts that do not fit him. But then, for
Luciano Pavarotti Inc., a multinational conglomerate, singing appears on its way to becoming a sideline in a continuing
manufacture of commercialism and hype." As early as the
middle 1980s the critic Peter G. Davis no longer accorded
Pavarotti the status of a serious artist, but offhandedly relegated him to the entertainer rubric in the *New Yorker* and
described his influence as one of the many riddles that mass
psychology gives rise to.

   In a word, the singer was floating on the clouds of fame
up to the rarefied regions of the gods. Criticism couldn't
touch him, at least as far as his mass appeal was concerned.

This is by no means meant to insinuate that the third decade of his career was nothing more than his downfall. There are very positive reviews during this period, even if they don't predominate. In a peculiar magazine with the curious title *Opera Fanatic* and dedicated to "lovers of expressive singing," Stefan Zucker, "the world's highest tenor," as he calls himself, describes the performance of *Ernani* as a "cornucopia of delights" and praises Pavarotti's singing as a "triumph." According to Zucker's description, Pavarotti's voice had become darker and thus more pleasant than it had been with its "unrelieved brightness of yore."

Zucker also described Pavarotti's first "classical concert" in the newly renovated Madison Square Garden before an audience of about twenty thousand people. The tenor began with "Questa o quella" and sounded "a little too mature for the Duke, his many extra breaths chopping up the phrasing." During the course of the evening these breath control problems seemed to fade away. His *passaggio* tones and his *acuti* were unconstricted, so that the audience "applauded *while* he sustained the final *La donna è mobile* interpolated B." About his rendition of the aria "Ah, sì, ben mio," Zucker wrote: "Pavarotti disgorged gorgeous tones and passable trills, but with about as much melancholy and pathos as his American Express commercial. He was stirring in 'Di quella pira' despite a half step transposition."[17] Most of the reviews, however, don't seem to say very much: general references ranging from "beautiful" singing or "strained and mindless vocalism," to the combination of "the highest ability with a penetrating sincerity and simplicity of being" and the "infatuating sweetness of high notes," to "the tender timbre of emotion." Precise descriptions of his voice, his technique, and his musical theatricality can be found in several of Will Crutchfield's reviews in the *New York Times*. What follows is a rather extensive quote from a review of Donizetti's *L'Elisir d'Amore*; it's a very telling piece, especially since this performance has been recorded in the meantime.[18]

> Except for three passages, Nemorino in *L'Elisir d'Amore* is nearly a perfect role for Luciano Pavarotti, who sang it . . . in the season's first performance of the work. It doesn't overtax the stamina or volume of his voice (both were more than ample); it isn't too high; it benefits from his lively, pointed diction, and it gives generous opportunities for both of his strongest traits as an actor—clowning and simple pathos. . . . The three passages are those that test musical imagination and elegance: "Chiedi all'aura" and "Adina, credimi" in the first act, "Una furtiva lagrima" in the second. These call for colors, contrasts and a kind of spiritual poetry that Mr. Pavarotti has never cultivated, and "Una furtiva lagrima" in particular was disappointingly square and static. But even here there was something to admire; he took the ornaments in "Chiedi all'aura" more smoothly than most other tenors of recent memory, and the taxing lines around what singers call "the break" in the other two were no problem at all. Indeed Mr. Pavarotti sounded all night like a tenor in fresh vocal prime; he has conceded very little to the passage of time or to the rigors of the heavy roles he has

undertaken. His one big concession was called to mind when he tried a high C and it turned out very thin.[19]

High praise, indeed, but not without a few discordant notes. Crutchfield, unquestionably one of the most knowledgeable critics of singing and acting, hints that Pavarotti is a singer with a moderate volume and a limited range (to B), and that his range of color is narrow and thus his potential for expressive nuance not very great. With this, then, Pavarotti is relegated back to the lyric field from which he originally came, and without any nasty undertones. Martin Mayer says that Pavarotti's voice has become more beautiful in the last ten years as a result of growing a bit darker and thereby attaining a grainier quality. He also feels that Pavarotti has overcome the problems he had in forming the high notes, which plagued his work during 1981 and 1982. There's no doubt that the somewhat darker sound more closely corresponds to the performances immortalized by Caruso, but this leads to a discussion of technique and the sound of a tenor voice, and that discussion is reserved for a later chapter.

THE METASTASIS OF FAME

The U.S. debut of the as yet relatively unknown Italian was a complete, enormous, and ingenious crescendo programmed to a great extent by the American Herbert Breslin; it culminated in the hysterical adoration of the world's crazed opera buffs. Breslin was . . . the perfect desktop director for the traditional machinations of the opera business. He's an accomplished master of the art of the threat—in this case, the castration of those journalists who don't dance to his tune. . . . Tibor Rudas had a completely different strategy in mind. "You're no mere opera singer anymore," was the seed the Hungarian planted in the Italian's ear, "you're a recording star. If you want to make sure your recordings keep on selling, you'll have to go to your audience the same way Sinatra and Neil Diamond go to theirs." The message was clear: get out of the Mets and the Scalas with their measly 2,000 or 2,300 paying operagoers and $8,000 to $10,000 token fees for an evening's work and go to the Central Parks, the sports arenas, and the summer stages. That's where the Pavarottis of the pop scene—Madonna and Prince and Michael Jackson—rake in the dough. Instead of Covent Garden, Britain's venerable temple of song, perform in Madison Square Garden, New York's gigantic acoustic pleasure dome; sooner play

F A M E

*Caesar's Palace than the Rome Opera, and rather than
settling for peanuts, go for the big bucks.*

KLAUS UMBACH, "Opera Bigwigs," in *Geldscheinsonate*

*I*n his book *Understanding Toscanini: How He Became an
American Culture God and Helped Create New Audiences for
Old Music*, Joseph Horowitz cites the example of the great
entrepreneur and circus manager Phineas Taylor Barnum,
who signed on Jenny Lind, the "Swedish Nightingale," in
1850–51. In his autobiography Barnum described this engage-
ment as "an enterprise never before or since equaled in mana-
gerial annals." Barnum was required to cough up $187,000
for this first tour—a colossal sum in those days. A reporter
for the *New York Herald* rose to new heights of hyperbole in
describing the singer's arrival in New York: it was "as
significant an event as the appearance of Dante, Tasso,
Raphael, Shakespeare, Goethe, Thorvaldsen, or Michael
Angelo"; she had "changed all men's ideas of music as much
as Bacon's inductive system revolutionized philosophy."[1]

Horowitz, obviously influenced by the Frankfurt school's
sociological approach to music and particularly by the ideas
of Theodor W. Adorno, sees this production of a cult surrounding a famous diva as the springboard for modern prac-

tices, for the establishment of a gigantic PR blitz intent upon commercializing the musical heritage that came into its own only with the help of Arturo Toscanini. In abstract terms, this was a matter of exchanging cause for effect: the music disappears behind the star who plays or sings it. As a consequence of the media age, this cult took on a new quality (*quantity* might be a more appropriate term) in Pavarotti's case. His voice became a universal sound, as ubiquitous as that "lite" music that drips like syrup from every loudspeaker: in department stores and hotel lobbies, in airplanes, taxis, and telephone holds. Italian restaurants serve pizza and pasta to the accompaniment of this voice, the tones of which are peddled in the consumer palaces of mass entertainment as crooning, spooning Italian good taste.

Our century has seen a number of singers who have performed with extraordinary success in the concert hall and who took side trips to the "muse of lite music." This is true for Caruso and Nellie Melba, for John McCormack and Feodor Chaliapin, and to a much greater extent for Richard Tauber or Benjamino Gigli, who held sway in the sports arena much the same way his political *fratelli* did with their rhetorical demagogy. Even Maria Callas and Mario del Monaco offered "aria evenings" in a pseudosophisticated circus atmosphere.

But these were intimate soirees compared to the Pavarotti shows. As a result of the efforts of Herbert Breslin, the singer gave his first recital in the John Gano Memorial Hall in

Liberty, Missouri, on February 1, 1973. His success encouraged him to perform additional solo concerts whose programs featured predominantly Italian songs, peppered here and there with a few operatic arias. By 1973–74 he had already given thirteen such concerts (not including the performances of Verdi's Requiem). The following season saw twice that number. Martin Mayer quotes the *London Times* critic John Higgins, who spoke of a triumph and of "two hours of total professionalism"—of a professional artistry without which such performances simply can't be "sold" for any length of time.[2] Obviously, the audience that turns up for this type of program is not one that wants to hear the *Winterreise* or the *Lieder eines fahrenden Gesellen*, even if they are to be sung by such luminaries as Dietrich Fischer-Dieskau or Christa Ludwig. In other words, the music is less of a draw than the singing celebrity.

During the course of a relatively few years the recitals became increasingly important. The 1977–78 season already featured more than thirty of them—and the effect was enhanced by Pavarotti's first coast-to-coast televised concert, *Live from Lincoln Center*, on February 12, 1978. Pavarotti sang before an audience of twelve million viewers (and listeners). Even today, with the eloquence of a born raconteur, he can still describe the paralyzing fear he experienced before this appearance: "I know that my audience loves me," he said, "but will it still love me after tonight?"[3] He thought, or talked himself into thinking, that a TV appearance would expose his fame to a type of test that didn't necessarily exist in an opera house or in a conventional recital hall: namely, that every constricted or unsteady note would be heard as a mistake or a failure. A television performance is different from a live presence onstage: what appears on the stage is a person, but what appears on the television screen is the fame of a celebrity that has long since disembodied itself from the man.

His success was phenomenal and cannot by any means be attributed solely to the results of a clever marketing strategy. If so-called super- or megastars could be produced in test tubes, there would surely be more of them. That's why Herbert Breslin, Pavarotti's first American manager, rejects the idea that he simply masterminded a brilliant marketing plan for the tenor. Breslin works for a number of outstanding artists without being able to produce the audience response for them that he can for Pavarotti. He chalks up Pavarotti's success in part to the singer's "remarkable artistry," in part to his "winning personality."[4] There's also another word for it, one coined by Jerzy Grotowski: "artist-courtesans."

This word is meant to be interpreted in a value-neutral way as being purely descriptive, as a metaphor for an ability to mesmerize, to entice, to play, to flirt, to persuade, without making it seem as if it were all a game or a screen. Even if Pavarotti is a bit cumbersome onstage—mainly because of his size—he is still an accomplished mime, and these talents serve him well, especially on TV. His facial features are still strong and well defined, his gaze alert and beaming, his smile charming; he can use his singing to flirt with his listeners and viewers, and he gives the impression that he loves his audience, that there is nothing in which he basks more happily than in the applause of the crowd.5

It was through the efforts of his agent Tibor Rudas, a P. T. Barnum of our day, that he finally found his way to the masses. The native Hungarian organizes every one of Pavarotti's appearances where the TV audience can hear the singer directly, or "live," as they say, without worrying about the implications of this term. For the past few years Rudas has been staging gala performances in which the singer appears "live" all over the world. Still, serious doubts remain as to whether the audience actually does experience a "live" voice and can reconstruct an acoustical image of the sound of a *vox humana*.6

Martin Mayer's book *Grandissimo Pavarotti* describes in detail the enormous investment in technical expertise necessary to produce these concerts, including the "peculiar attention" that is paid "to the possibilities and potentials of technical amplification." Rudas-Pavarotti Enterprises employs James Lock, the recording director of Decca in London, the sound effects specialist Roger Ganz of the San Francisco Opera, and the San Francisco sound engineer Drew Serb, conceivably the world's best team when it comes to producing sound in a huge hall—a sound, moreover, that the singer himself can control by means of two small loudspeaker monitors (which is only possible if he stands completely still) and that the audience perceives as a natural tone.[7] All the same, to the ears of this listener it's a different sound from what emanates from the loudspeakers of a hi-fi set. In these huge arenas it's difficult to hear the coloration of a voice, its tonal nuances, as precisely as one can on a recording, and in spite of all efforts at amplification, one gets the impression of a disproportion. The true dimension of the voice and the exact definition of the note, both of which can be experienced fully in an opera house, are hard to pick up in such an environment.

Even so, the appearances of the singer occasion enormous tension and excitement. They are events of a special ilk: they employ myths and marketing strategies, mass psychology and changes in the cultural scene to pander to the big business of satisfying aesthetic needs with a cultural aura. It's besotted shortsightedness to think that these musical mutations and this metastasizing of popular myths[8] could be arrested or resisted with the means or the verbal weapons of cultural criticism. Whoever believes in the efficacy of cultural criticism, as Hans Magnus Enzensberger once said in an almost cynical way, has only himself to blame.[9]

The Voice of
the Tenor

Un nido di memorie in fondo a l'anima cantava

un giorno, ed ein con vere lacrime scrisse, e i

singhiozzi il tempo gli battevano!

RUGGIERO LEONCAVALLO
prologue to Pagliacci

LAUGH, CLOWN!

*Don't you know that a tenor is not a denizen of this
world, he is a world in himself.*

HECTOR BERLIOZ, *Evenings with the Orchestra*

Stendhal, the novelist and passionate music lover, a
biographer of Gioachino Rossini, expressed the fear
that someday only a very few would find pleasure in conversations about dancers or singers. "In the twentieth century
people will be talking only about politics; and instead of
applauding Marianna Conti, they will be reading the *Morning Chronicle*."[1] Stendhal feared a brave new world devoid of
culture, whose public life would be kept completely in check
by bureaucrats. What never even entered his mind was the
possibility that opera, too—this theater of improbability, of
suspended logic—would be absorbed in the new world of
mundane business transactions and rationalized aesthetics.
Gone, gone for good are the days when one could be carried
away by a miracle of fantasy, by the sublime artificiality of the
evirati. The former castrati practiced an art unequaled ever

since, using "their incorporeal voices at the sublime peak of coloratura singing" to fill the hall with "abstract images of stylized but most passionate erotic feelings."[2]

There was no place for the tenor in this older form of opera, at least no featured role. According to Luca Fontana, the myth of the tenor first appeared

> when Italian opera had sunk to its lowest depths of decadence; when the petite bourgeoisie, nourished by good or bad verist literature, by nationalist myths and easily accessible materialist aesthetics, appropriated the theater stalls as well as the boxes of the old opera houses. Two one-act operas—beloved by German and American audiences, regarded with great suspicion by Italians, and abhorred by composers—characterize the emergence of this new taste: *Cavalleria Rusticana* and *I Pagliacci*. It was supposed to be verismo in music—wildly popular, as I said, in Germany and America, because they reduce the whole Mediterranean myth ultimately to the level of touristic kitsch. Even the new vocal line they introduced aims to integrate into song all of those natural and idiosyncratic data that the Italian school had labored so hard and so long for the past two centuries to eliminate: the strains, the screams, the mimesis of dialogic declamation so characteristic of naturalistic theater.[3]

There are a number of reasons why the myth of the tenor originates with the person of Enrico Caruso. The tenor tradition reached its highest point in him, and his recordings opened the door to mass audiences. The myth goes back to him because his conservative musical estate dominated the following four decades at least and literally forced his successors to adopt what Fontana bitterly and correctly dubs the veristic approach, a manner of singing that can hardly be described as a style. "Caruso is the standard," Pavarotti told me, "against which all later tenors have measured themselves, and he is the model from which they have all learned."

Does this apply to Pavarotti, too—the man who has become a living legend like no other, the focus of cover stories in *Newsweek* and *Time*, the star of coast-to-coast American television broadcasts, the man who sings in Olympic stadiums and public arenas, on summer stages and in Central Park, the man who conquered the British hit parade with Puccini's "Nessun dorma" and who, wrapped in starry banners and sporting a cowboy hat, led the Columbus Day parade? Pavarotti, a man no longer simply famous, but renowned for his fame? This mighty man from Modena has long since dissolved into his own myth. Coffee-table books portray him as Grandissimo Pavarotti, and the effect is no less monstrous than that of the story in *Der Spiegel*, the German equivalent of *Time*, where he stoops to the level of a gastronomic comic insatiably pursuing fettucini and rigatoni and even more insatiably transforming musical notes into banknotes. The ethical, sexual, cultural, and economic frustrations of the 1950s, projected as they were onto Maria Callas by the redressing processes of the yellow press, assumed the guise of moral indignation not only against her but against the common man in general, and today's *tenoris-simo* has to bear the brunt of similar attacks.

Like Maria Callas, Pavarotti, too, is a living legend—and that means, just as in the case of the Greek singer, that he was robbed of his history and transformed into a monstros-ity. The only problem is that today, unlike the eighteenth century, such a *monstre* is no longer *sacré*. Pavarotti's story doesn't begin in 1961 in Reggio nell'Emilia, where he made his debut; it's as old as Italian opera itself. And there is no one with whom one can better discuss this history than Luciano Pavarotti himself, always supposing you want to talk to him about singing the way Stendhal described it and aren't waiting for those punch lines and impudent remarks that he, shrewd by nature as well as by experience with the media, tosses off with as much confidence as he does his *acuti*. Does he have any other choice than to be a double agent, a tenor and an actor portraying a tenor? A tenor and a clown? An actor playing the role of clown? After all, hasn't the expres-sion "as dumb as a tenor" embedded itself in our vernacular as solidly as a rusty nail?

Pavarotti is more clever than most of the people who make jokes and jabs at his expense; he's anything but the brainless blockhead he's made out to be. Nor is he, as Fontana says, the figure of fun that many people, mostly in America, deprecatingly portray him to be. He may be a star as far as his social status is concerned, but his persona forces him to play the role of the buffoon, of the comedian, who—laugh,

Pagliaccio!—has to act out a farce not only to please the public but also to escape from it.

Pavarotti plays his game with the public with the charm of a lady's man intent on pleasing. But he doesn't leave it at that. He uses the frequently inane and pointless questions that pop up in conversations and interviews to get in a punch line no less pithy than the ones that pepper scripts like that of *The Great Caruso*, a 1951 movie with Mario Lanza in the title role. He has a number of prefabricated answers for the question of why so much fuss is made about the ominous high C, each one finely tuned to the situation at hand. "An evening doesn't easily recover from a botched C," he once told me with a wrinkled brow, and his facial expression seems to say that he finds it ridiculous—just as Adorno does in his essay on the fetishization of music and the diminishing ability to listen.4 Or else he confesses to having "a mystical feeling" while singing, "like taking off in a trance," and to feeling far removed from this earth for the ecstatic eternity of six or eight seconds. Sometimes he peers at the interviewer in an admonishing way and says in the tone of a professor who has to explain yet again something he has repeated a hundred times before, "My dear friend"—and the "dear" sounds like a warning—"the tenor voice is not a natural one. It is artificial. It has little in common with a man's normal speaking voice; the natural voice of a man is the baritone. When I wake up in the morning, my voice isn't just there; I have to find it, I have to formally construct it like a sculpture . . . and this day after day."5

He'll occasionally treat an interviewer or conversation partner as an insider ("Okay, between us *savanti* of bel canto") and arrange a *tour d'horizon*, will talk about Caruso's recordings and about all the other tenors his father suggested as (better) models for him whenever he gave a debut performance somewhere. Although eclectic in this respect, Pavarotti knows well the recordings of Aureliano Pertile and Tito Schipa, of Benjamino Gigli and Jussi Björling, of Giuseppe di Stefano and Mario del Monaco, of Franco Corelli and Nicolai Gedda—and you can't shake him by asking about Giovanni Battista Rubini or Giovanni Matteo Mario, the tenors of the romantic age, whose parts he also sings. He never loses his cool because, like a politician, he answers only the questions he wants to answer, without being so clumsy about it as to embarrass the reporter or to make him feel he asked a dumb or inappropriate question. When he looks at the interviewer in his admonishing way and addresses him with "My dear friend," right away you know that he means to say, "Of course you're right . . . but do you have any idea how complicated this profession is? How unendingly difficult it is to live up to the demands, the expectations of the public?"

Luciano Pavarotti is famous not only because he's so extraordinarily famous, but because he feeds the amazing legend of his worldwide reputation with tidbits, as it were, from a *Thousand and One Nights* of vocal history. He cites all sorts of episodes, anecdotes, facts, and current myths that end up in the magazine stories as "factoids," to use the current

American expression for a combination of facts and fiction or even, what is worse, that manipulation of facts that ends up producing mere fiction. Because they are taken out of their original context as well as historical setting and are thus deprived of their objective significance as well as their aesthetic framework, these factoids become as random as the anecdotes they give rise to and that are said to be, if not true, then at least well contrived.

The voice of a tenor, according to Pavarotti, is not a natural but an artificial one. What are we supposed to glean from that? One explanation that deserves more than a cursory dismissal as being vulgarly materialistic or fetishistic has to do with the sensuous effect the tenor voice has on its listeners. This quality combines the fullness, strength, and energy of a man's voice with the charm and chaste enchantment of the choirboy, thus enabling it to appeal to and elicit particularly "the woman's favor." The effect of this combination stands and falls "with the possession of an absolute, ever-reliable, and translucent upper register, which in the case of a lyric tenor can reach up to C, C sharp, and D, in the case of the youthful hero and the dramatic tenor to C, and with heroic tenors at least to B flat."[6] Nothing, absolutely nothing—"An evening doesn't easily recover from a botched high C"—can compensate for or camouflage problems in producing the *do di petto*, the *ut de poitrine*, the high C.

Let's return to the effect the theater critic Edward Gordon Craig calls "physiological contagion." "There is nothing

more exciting than a great high tenor sound," Joan Sutherland was quoted as having said in the extensive story that
appeared in 1976 in *Newsweek*—a story modeled after the
"factoid" piece described above. "It's largely an artificial
sound, since men usually speak in the baritone register.
Whether it's Enrico Caruso and Richard Tucker or Kenny
Baker and Dennis Day, the sound of the tenor conveys a
perverse virility in its combination of high-pitched boyish-
ness and manly strength."[7] It's because of this effect that
tenors have long since proved to be not only what Americans
call the best box office draws; they are also looked upon as
eccentric and odd—as creatures, in other words, that are
comprehensible only in being a world unto themselves. That
"every talented person possesses the intelligence of his natural calling,"[8] and that the singer's thoughts revolve as if
obsessed around this strange being in his throat, is only too
soon forgotten in light of the frequently eccentric behavior of
these usually small and compact men, of whom innumerable
stories (more than *mille e tre*) tell. "That high C is for Mr.
Schonberg," the tenor Michele Molese cried out, stepping up
to the footlights; it was his emotional release against the *New
York Times* critic who reproached the tenor of the New York
City Opera with having produced "squeezed" top notes.[9]
This is anecdotal material confirming a statement Arturo
Toscanini made regarding the number of vibrations required
to produce the higher tones: since the basic oscillation of
vocal cords with a length of two centimeters singing a high

C tuned to the concert pitch of 440 Hertz is 523.2 oscillations per second, such a tone would have to lead to brain damage among tenors. Stranger yet, and the material for an antiquated story, is the fact that the tenor Giuseppe Anselmi (1876–1929), one of Enrico Caruso's major rivals, concluded his will with the words "I leave my heart to the city of Madrid."[10]

He didn't mean this in any metaphorical sense, or as some sort of homage to the Teatro Real and its audience, which had greeted him so wildly and wouldn't have traded him for two Carusos; the truth is that he wanted his heart preserved like a reliquary at the site of his triumphs—which is also what happened, in the end. Anselmi told his admirers that he always said a prayer before the statue of Christ prior to a performance and that, in keeping with an old superstition, he made sure he touched a long iron rod. Similar stories have been told about Pavarotti, too, including the one about his always looking around for a bent nail before stepping out onstage. Why should he deny this, when such an eccentricity fits in so well and lends narrative color to the tales of today's heroes much the way Giacomo Puccini's brief question sums up the essence of the myth surrounding the young Caruso: "Who sent you? God?"[11]

concerned, their success, their fortunes, their whims, and their personal idiosyncrasies, the anecdotes about tenors are dry bones in comparison to the legends that tell of the experiences and dangers, the glory and the misery suffered by the *evirati*. The last major castrato of opera history was Giovanni Battista Velluti, for whom Giacomo Meyerbeer composed a major role in *Il Crociato in Egitto*, which premiered in Venice in 1824.[5] The last castrato of any eminence to be associated with the Sistine Chapel was Domenico Mustapha (1829–1912), who hailed from Turkey and served as the director of the choir of the Sistine Chapel until 1902. The memoirs of Emma Calvé contain a most beautiful epitaph for this singer. She had heard notes emanating from Mustapha's upper ranges that struck her as "strange, sexless tones, superhuman, uncanny." She asked him how she might learn to produce such divinely and bewitchingly beautiful sounds. He replied that it was quite simple, really: all she had to do was practice singing with her mouth shut for ten years. In her memoirs, Calvé recalls her initial discouragement, and how she conquered it and did indeed begin the exercise. Two years later she discovered what she called her "fourth voice," and it can still be heard on several of her recordings.[6]

The castrato's reign rested on the stylized art form known as *opera seria*, with its mythical themes and its all-pervasive glorification of imperious virtues in the era of absolutism. Of course, the musical language in which they sang was not called bel canto—the concept would have been a tautology at a time when "expression" in the modern sense of the word was not what people wanted from singing, but rather the artificial beauty of an elaborately formal and formulaic language. Yet that name or concept, first coined probably toward the end of the nineteenth century, is truly appropriate to the stylized *opera seria*.[7]

It was not until the middle of the eighteenth century that the tenor was assigned a new role, the "modern" one of the lover. This shift was made possible by the emergence of *opera buffa*, which took its themes neither from mythology nor from the glorification of sovereign autonomy and grace, but rather from that real, if sometimes unrealistically represented, life that we know from the *commedia*. It would be going too far in this regard to speak of the life and influence of Angelo Amorevoli, the Venetian who sang with eminent technical bravura and a presumably relatively dark voice and who was responsible for Italy's first reconsideration and higher appreciation of the tenor.[8] It would be going just as far to tell of the famous Frenchman Pierre Jélyotte, an alto who, according to all witnesses, overwhelmed his audience, and particularly his female audience, with his clear, soft, and silvery timbre and his graceful manner.

If Amorevoli can be said to have been an agile tenor-baritone, a *tenore baritonale d'agilità*, two other singers who hailed from the region around Bergamo toward the end of the eighteenth century were by all accounts capable of fantastic flights into the higher ranges. These were the father-

and-son team of Giacomo and Giovanni David, and it was
the son who carried away his audience, as well as the Rossini
biographer Stendhal, "by the evocative gracefulness of his
elegant, pure, and full-toned voice" until they "grew mindless of all else in the world."9 Both Davids were tenor-bari-
tones who switched to the falsetto to accelerate their flights
to the vocal stratosphere. The same can be said of the elegant Andrea Nozarri, the expressive Manuel Garcia, or Nicola Tacchinardi, renowned for his dramatic talents, not to
mention the mighty Domenico Donzelli, who sang the role
of Pollione in the premiere performance of Bellini's *Norma*
and had already lent rather powerful vocal stature to the
dramatic tenor in Rossini's *Otello.*10

According to Henry Fothergill Chorley (and this is the
testimony of one of the greatest *savanti*), Donzelli possessed
"one of the most mellifluous robust low tenor voices ever
heard—a voice which had never by practice been made
sufficiently flexible to execute Signor Rossini's operas as they
were written." The singer himself, however, "even in this
respect, was accomplished and finished if compared with the
violent persons who have succeeded him. . . . The volume of
Donzelli's rich and sonorous voice was real and not forced.
When he gave out its high notes, there were no misgivings
as to the peril of his blood vessels; and hence his reign on the
Italian stage was thrice as long as that of any of the worse-
endowed, worse-trained folk who have since adopted the
career of forcible tenor."11

This description corresponds exactly to a review in the Viennese *Allgemeine Musikalische Zeitung* from 1823. This article states that in his role as Otello, Donzelli sang the high A in a full chest voice without ever using the falsetto, while Signor David sparkled as Roderigo with the falsetto in the highest tessitura and even sang an F″. The score indicates that Otello has to hit many A's and even B flats, especially in the *fioritura*, whereas the part of Roderigo demands not only a number of high C's but a dozen high D's as well. The role of Iago was also written with a tenor in mind. What we now know as the modern baritone was practically unknown then, for it was Rossini who created it with his Figaro, even demanding the G′. Knowing all this, we can imagine that Garcia's voice reached its limits with this tone.

The composers considered it an absolute matter of course to match their musical demands with the individual singers and their capabilities. In fact, Mozart had no problem with stuffing the "mellifluous throat of Mme. Cavaliere" with "sliced noodles," which is the term he used to describe the inserted coloraturas. He even confessed that he loved to tailor a role to Ludwig Fischer as one would a "well-made garment," and Rossini or Bellini were no different in this regard. Donzelli sent a letter to the composer of *Norma* with a precise description of his voice together with advice concerning what one would today call the *passaggio*: the shift between registers.

If one were to speak metaphorically of the epochs of tenor singing, Donzelli marks the end of the Bronze Age. The dawn of the Silver Age can actually be traced back to a specific evening when one of the first romantic heroes stepped onto the operatic stage. He was a hero from the realm of sensuality and passion, who sang of yearning and of tender, unfulfilled, and unrequited love:

Nel furor delle tempeste
nelle stragi del pirata
quell'imagine adorata
sie presenta al mio pensier . . .

The scene is the Teatro alla Scala in Milan, October 27, 1827: the premiere performance of Vincenzo Bellini's *Il Pirata* with Giovanni Battista Rubini (1795–1854) singing the title role and Henriette Méric-Lalande as Imogene. The melodies that Rubini sang and continued to sing were of such beauty that they elicited the praise of romantic poets from Alfred de Musset and Byron to Baudelaire, Verlaine, and Gide, who described them as being "invincibly sad" and "desperate."[12] Rubini must have sung with melting evocativeness and a timbre of androgynous beauty, thereby strengthening in the highest position the soft and sensuous neutral tones produced by the Davids. He lent them glowing brilliance and lyric sensitivity—in other words, the expressive coloring that one hardly ever finds in the veiled music of the younger Rossini.[13]

In his *Thirty Years' Musical Recollections* Chorley writes: "There never was an artist who seemed so thoroughly and

intensely to enjoy his own singing—a persuasion which cannot fail to communicate itself to audiences. . . . As a singer
and nothing but a singer he is the only man of his class who
deserves to be named in these pages as an artist of genius. No
one in my experience . . . so entirely enchanted our public so
long as a shred of voice was left to him; no one is more
affectionately remembered."[14] Henry Pleasants feels that in
terms of technique, Rubini, although a romantic singer, was
a descendant of the great castrati Pacchierotti and Cres-
centini, Ansani and Raaff, and that his art developed primarily in that cantabile style of singing that, according to
Stendhal, emitted the "mystic powers of the human voice"
like an opiate. In the romantic period, this was perceived as
a combination of the "transports of delirium and rapture."

The following anecdote speaks for itself: both Franz Liszt
and Frédéric Chopin admitted they learned the art of pianistic
phrasing by listening to the leading singers of their day,
mainly Rubini and the great Giuditta Pasta. The modern variation of this theme can be found in the person of the pianist
Vladimir Horowitz, who, as he has frequently said, spent his
whole life listening to the recordings of Giusepppi Anselmi
and especially those of Mattia Battistini in order to study their
rhythmic nuances and the finesse of their phrasing. This is an
art that is being neglected by precisely those who have the
most to learn from it: the singers of Italian romantic opera.

Chorley on Rubini: "The tradition of his method died
with him."[15] So much space has been devoted to this singer

(who died in 1854) because he sang two of the most important roles in Pavarotti's repertoire in their respective premiere performances: Elvino in *La Sonnambula* and Arturo in *I Puritani*. Two other tenors deserve mention in this regard as well, for their brilliant interpretations were also pivotal for Pavarotti's development. One is Adolphe Nourrit (1802–39), for whom Gioachino Rossini wrote the roles of Néocles in *Le Siège de Corinth*, Aménophis in *Moïse et Pharaon*, Arnold in *Guillaume Tell*, and the title role in *Le Comte Ory*. Daniel-François-Esprit Auber wrote the role of Masaniello in *La Muette de Portici* and *Gustave III* for him as well. Nourrit was also the tenor who sang in the premiere performance of Giacomo Meyerbeer's *Robert le Diable* and *Les Huguenots*. The other tenor is Gilbert-Louis Duprez, who sang the title role in the premiere performance of Hector Berlioz's *Benvenuto Cellini* and to whom the composer later dedicated an ironic "astronomical study" in his collection of essays *Evenings with the Orchestra*.

One would be hard pressed to overstate the position Adolphe Nourrit occupies in the history of opera; according to Pleasants, he was the embodiment of the "greatest singing actor among all the dramatic tenors of opera history."[16] Not only is the number of roles he was the first to sing extraordinary, but even more impressive is the way the quality of his singing managed to convey the enduring substance of a role to the consciousness of his contemporary audience during the very first performance. "Indeed, until Verdi and Wagner came along," Pleasants tells us, "it could be said that Nourrit, virtually single handed, had made a repertoire for the dramatic tenor."[17] He succeeded in establishing a place for the acting type rather the way Wilhelmine Schröder-Devrient did for Wagner: a singing actor who was also an accomplished acting singer. The Italian manner was alien to him. Influenced by the great theatrical actor François-Joseph Talma, Nourrit was concerned not only with the beauty of tone production, the charms of the cantabile, and the finesses of *canto spianato*, but also with the nuances of drama and dialogue, the suggestive gestures of pantomine, the meaning in the text and in declamation—in short, with all of what Wagner described in his *Opera and Drama* as the representation of music via the spirit of drama.

Nourrit withdrew when the Italian-trained Gilbert-Louis Duprez was not only engaged at the Grand Opéra in Paris but also allowed to debut as Arnold in *Guillaume Tell*. Nourrit spent some time touring the French provinces, all the while resentful that his less subtle but vocally stronger rival had found such favor among the opera public. Finally, in a depressed and confused mental state, he took his life in Naples on March 8, 1839. The memorial service was held in Paris on April 24, when Frédéric Chopin played the organ in the church of Notre-Dame-du-Mont "with a plaintive sound, as soft as an echo from another world" (George Sand).[18]

THE SEISMIC SHOCK

Duprez today electrified us all. What daring! A terrifying old lion! How he hurled his guts in the audience's face! For those are no longer notes that one hears. They are the explosions of a breast crushed by an elephant's foot! That's his own blood, his own life, that he is squandering to entice from the public those cries of "Bravo!" with which the Romans honored the dying gladiator.

GUSTAVE ROGER on Gilbert-Louis Duprez as Otello
in Rossini's opera, 1849

*I*t wasn't the creative artist and eminent dramatic actor Adolphe Nourrit, but Gilbert-Louis Duprez who was to mark the most significant turning point in the history of singing, and he did it with the sound the American singer Stefan Zucker described as the "seismic shocker."[1] According to the descriptions of Berlioz, an objective critic despite his irony, Duprez must have been a reliable deliverer of the high notes for quite a while, even if he was a careless musician. He dazzled his audiences with energetically attacked full tones in the high ranges, but as early as 1838 he was already incapable of sustaining the high G for three bars at the end of the phrase "Je chanterais gaîment" in Cellini's "Sur les monts les plus sauvages." Berlioz also reports that Duprez sang an F instead of a G flat in "Asile héréditaire" and, when it was brought to his attention, is said to have retorted, "That note puts me out. It bothers me."[2]

Even the reports of reliable chroniclers can give a false deposition, especially in the case of those singers who found themselves somehow out of tune with their times. Before Duprez came to France and to the critical ears of Berlioz, he already had ten years of singing in Italy behind him, including the role of Edgardo in the premiere performance of Gaetano Donizetti's *Lucia di Lammermoor*. Judging by the final scene, he must have been as elegant a singer as he was moving. In 1831 he sang the part of Arnoldo in the Italian premiere of *Guglielmo Tell*, and this task called for a heroic effort on his part. In this work, unlike his early Neapolitan operas, *exempla classica* of Italian classicism, Rossini is aiming at that intensification of orchestral and vocal means best described as *expression outrée*.[3] Not only does the part of Arnold lie in the highest tessitura, but exposed tones in ensembles have to be sung as well and have to be sustained in full and dramatic projection. It is the first hybrid tenor role in the history of opera.[4]

In the early years of his career, however, it cost Duprez a great deal of effort to hold his own even in easy roles. In his

Souvenirs d'un Chanteur he reports that he needed the deepest concentration and all the power of his will to produce something like a sonorous figure for the role of Arnold, and most of all to master the truly fear-inspiring climactic phrase in the *stretta* after "Asile héréditaire," rising from G over B flat and B to the sustained C. As mentioned above, Duprez did not like the sound at all; critics, and not only Berlioz, found fault with Duprez's lax intonation as well as his lack of agility, possibly due to the dark monochrome of his voice, which may also have compromised his inflection. In pointing out his defects, these critics also recalled the art of the *voix mixte*, which had allowed Nourrit to rise as high as C sharp (demanded in the duet of the second act) and to do so with no visible sign of effort. But the echo of that *ut de poitrine* caused a quake in the world of opera and in that of tenors.

This was the beginning of specialization for tenors. Rubini was considered the standard for the type of light, lyric singer (*tenore di grazia*), Duprez served as the model for the dramatic *tenori stentorei*. Rubini was followed by Napoleone Moriani (with whom Giuseppina Strepponi had two children before she became Giuseppe Verdi's wife), by the wonderful Stefano Matteo de Candia, known as Mario and famous for his melting manner and mellifluous tones "that could charm a soul in purgatory,"[5] by the elegant and masterful Angelo Masini, and finally by the artistic perfectionist Fernando de Lucia, whose numerous recordings give us a clear picture of the art of a long-lost and long-forgotten era of singing.

The most prominent members of the ancestral line of heroic tenors include, after Nourrit and Duprez, Enrico Tamberlik (1820–89) and Gaetano Fraschini, one of the young Verdi's singers known as the "tenor of curses." On the one hand, Tamberlik sang the French repertoire of Nourrit and Duprez, on the other the roles of Donzelli, especially Rossini's Otello and Bellini's Pollione. Moreover, he was considered the unequaled interpreter of Verdi's Manrico, Ernani, the Duke, and Don Alvaro. He even sang the role of Mestizen in the premiere performance of *La Forza del Destino* in Saint Petersburg. It was Tamberlik who interpolated the high C into the *stretta* in *Il Trovatore*; today a singer would have a hard time defending his decision not to sing it, even if he tried to justify the omission by claiming fidelity to the original work. The range of Tamberlik's voice must have been extraordinary. To the great displeasure of the composer, Tamberlik substituted a full-voiced C sharp for an A in the finale of Rossini's *Otello*; according to an 1877 report by the Londoner P. G. Hurst, Tamberlik's "famous C sharp" rang out "with such extraordinary power and freshness that a repetition of the passage was demanded and granted."[6] Verdi proved to be less sensitive than Rossini about the high C's in the *stretta*, which the audience greeted with wild acclaim: he felt it wasn't the composer's task to argue with the public.

We can get a more precise picture of the vocal style as well
as the sound of these singers by listening to the recordings of
Verdi's first Otello—Francesco Tamagno (1851–1905), even if
they are those of a singer with heart disease who had long
since withdrawn from the stage after an exhausting career.
Tamagno was known as the *vociferatore*, the *suonatore*, who,
to borrow a phrase from William James Henderson, hurled
his *acuti* with "the force of an eight-inch mortar" into the
theater stalls. The director Leopoldo Mugnone was on hand
when Tamagno added five C's to the "Corian" *stretta* in
Guglielmo Tell. Less admiring are the commentaries concerning his musical and acting abilities—and this whether
they take the form of remarks in Verdi's letters or critiques
of George Bernard Shaw or even the judgment of future
generations.[7]

It is precisely those people who reproach the general public with cult worship for the unsophisticated pleasure they
take in high notes for their own sake who have evidently and
intentionally failed to hear the marvelously veiled and softly
phrased passages in the recordings of this "great old roarer,"
as Tamagno was frequently called. Granted, his performance
can be described as neither graceful nor elegant, neither soft
nor melting, but Henry Pleasants' opinion that Tamagno
was "incapable of subtle singing" is difficult to accept.[8] The
brilliance of his singing lay in the concentration and compression of a cleanly focused tone and not, as was the case
with later *tenori di forza* for example, in the pouring out of a

broad stream of turbid and dark sound. The latter is all too frequently available (and unbearable) in the singing of the most famous of all postwar Otellos, Mario del Monaco.[9]

It goes without saying that a musical composition can never demand more of singing technique or vocal style than is either available or possible. In the seventeenth, more so in the eighteenth, and even as late as the beginning of the nineteenth century, composers wrote for the singers of their day. In addition, however, they expected the art of vocal improvisation to provide a kind of musical surplus: ornaments and graces, the addition of *abbellimenti*, the embellishment of musical speech.[10] In short, they expected the eloquence that results naturally from the sovereign mastery of vocal gestures and formulas and that lends a pictorial element to the musical impression. One need only listen to such singers as Victor Maurel, Mattia Battistini, or Fernando de Lucia to hear what I mean. That art was still available and developing under Verdi—with the emphasis on *still*. A few examples will illustrate my point: Iago's "Era la notte," Falstaff's "Quand' ero paggio," some of the Duke's lyric recitative passages or cadenzas, as well as the composer's taut cantabile passages.[11]

The vocal tradition reached its peak with two singers in their prime around the turn of the century: Jean de Reszke (1850–1925) and Enrico Caruso (1873–1921). De Reszke can be heard only on a few of the legendary Mapleson cylinders (if attention to this type of acoustic archaeology can be described as hearing).[12] Even so, it's easy to see how he came to be known as an aristocratic anachronism already in his own day. He not only acted the part of hero or nobleman or lover—Radames, Vasco da Gama, Lohengrin, Walther von Stolzing, Siegfried, Tristan, Romeo—but became their very incarnation and idealization as well. Cosima Wagner, who had already introduced the "Bayreuth bark" (Shaw) to the Wagnerian singers, came to appreciate the beauty of Lohengrin's songs through de Reszke's performance. He easily—or should one say frivolously?—rejected the heroic pose. In Verdi's *Aïda* he simply omitted Radames' ballad because his voice was "not yet sufficiently warmed up," and when he sang his first Otello in London in 1891, George Bernard Shaw complained of a "petulant laziness" in his acting. "He viewed art from the standpoint of a man of exquisite refinement," William James Henderson tells us in *The Art of Singing*, and in so doing he appealed to the moderately conservative taste of that New York society that transformed the round of theaters into a "diamond horse-shoe."[13]

De Reszke was not only the "greatest Romeo who ever stepped on stage" (Henderson), but also an ideal Faust, Des Grieux, Raoul, Jean de Leyden. As an incomparable stylist of the French repertoire he sang only one role that can be attributed to the (then) modern repertoire: Don José in *Carmen*. Even so, he could hardly have been able to reach the same heights of emotion as did his successor at the Met,

Enrico Caruso. Caruso's art not only represented the culmination of what has generally or even meaninglessly come to
be known as bel canto; to quote Luciano Pavarotti, the man
himself set his own definitive stamp on "the singing of all
tenors of the Italian school."

THE END OF PERFECTION

Most imitators are attracted by the inimitable.

MARIE VON EBNER-ESCHENBACH

*T*he four decades following Caruso witnessed no further development. That being the case, a brief examination of Caruso and his repertoire will serve as the key to an understanding of the singers who came after him and, not lastly, to Pavarotti himself.

What follows is the obituary William James Henderson, the most competent of all contemporaries, wrote following Caruso's death. It appeared in the August 3, 1921, issue of the *New York Sun*:

His voice was originally purely lyric, a smooth, mellow, sonorous but not heavy voice, but beyond all question the most beautiful tenor heard by any living operagoer. His early successes in New York were in lyric roles in such operas as *La Bohème, Tosca, L'Elisir d'Amore, La Gioconda*, with occasional excursions into the more dramatic realms of *Aïda*. In those days his voice had the charm of a velvety mellowness coupled with richness and sustained equality quite incomparable. When the years have made the perspective clearer the most sensitive among music lovers will recall his delivery of the great arias "Cielo e mar" and "Furtiva lagrima" as the loftiest flights of his lyric genius. His ambition, however, was to shine in more heroic parts and in the course of a few years he developed that powerful medium register which he used with such brilliant declamatory effect in *Samson and Dalila* and *La Juive* and *Le Prophète*. In doing this he sacrificed something of the transparent purity of tone which was one of the most beautiful traits of his earlier singing. He acquired a new manner of attack, more vigorous and explosive, but lost nothing of the pealing brilliancy of his high tones. . . . No other tenor remembered by living operagoers had so beautiful a voice. No other had a better technic. But in range of conception, in ability to dramatize ideas and emotions with the voice, in power to give interpretations complete illusion, some others excelled him. In sincerity, in fervor, in devotion to his art, he was the peer of any opera singer in history.[1]

In his further remarks concerning the *actor*, Henderson emphasizes that Caruso, completely unlike de Reszke, made a "bourgeois" impression in the role of Raoul, and that his portrayal of Des Grieux was anything but that of a French cavalier. We would be doing him a disservice to trace this deficiency back to his personal origins, for the singer's dramatic energy and creativity were such as to make him a first-class actor in the course of his New York years. Yet he no longer played the parts of those lovers who, like Edgardo or Elvino or Arturo, do nothing more than dream and sing of love and suffer the pains of heartbreak. As a contemporary of the verists he sang of the battle of the sexes, and his voice, this rich, sensuous, and impassioned voice, became a kind of seismograph of sensuality and sexuality. There is a recording of "O Lola" from *Cavalleria Rusticana* sung in a Sicilian dialect that causes one's senses to reel and sounds like a sonorous moan of ecstasy.

Caruso combined the classical technique of voice training—the perfect bowing, as it were, of a warm and expressive cello by the hand of a Casals—with the sensuous gestures of a modern Latin lover. He imbues his vocal gestures with more psychological realism, his emotional expression with more heartrending sorrow, than anyone else. There is a painful catch of breath in his attack, and a dynamic culmination in his accentuation that delivers a kind of vocal white heat. He has full control over the burning *fuoco sacro*—and, in his greatest moments, over an emotional outpouring that can be appreciated only in Orphic terms. It simply can't be described or explained in any other way.

The art of Italian tenor singing and bel canto is said to have reached its perfection in Caruso, whom many considered an anachronism, especially with regard to his musical style. The *canto fiorito*, which profited most by the embellishments of bel canto, soon lost its bloom; the fact that Arturo Toscanini kept the recordings of Fernando de Lucia only to ensure himself a good laugh every day speaks for itself. Since

tenors such as Alessandro Bonci and even John McCormack
paled in comparison to Caruso, the successors of the Neapolitan began to make use of the arsenal of gestures and
affects that Caruso had stocked. And they turned to the
sound recording. Caruso was the one who transformed the
record into an instrument; his successors made it the medium
of vocal leveling.

It may be that Benjamino Gigli, to take but one example,
was indeed an "angelic tenor," as Rodolfo Celletti maintained;[2] perhaps, as an entire chorus of other admirers and
critics proclaim, he did indeed possess the most beautiful
lyric tenor voice of the century. I don't agree; I think he
suffers from too much of an infantile "Maaaaammmmmaaa"
complex that caters to popular sentimentality, on the one
hand, and on the other, from an exaggerated emotionalism
that lends itself all too easily to political misuse. This is
precisely what happened to the singer himself, who sold out
to the Fascists. Aureliano Pertile (1885–1952), Toscanini's
favorite tenor, wasn't immune to this temptation, either. His
performances are saturated not only with verismo but also
with the exaggerated rhetorical screaming of political dema-
gogues from the darkest past. Tito Schipa and Giacomo
Lauri-Volpi were the only ones to link up with the traditions
of the *tenore di grazia* and of the romantic tenors of Bellini
and Donizetti without simultaneously currying that favor
among the general public that Gigli, the "pied piper of Re-
canati," enjoyed. Even Jussi Björling (1911–60), one of the

most brilliant tenor voices of the century, spent his whole life contending with Mario del Monaco for the admiration he was granted only after his death. Unlike practically all Italians, the singing Swede "with the icy purity" (Celletti) refused to imitate Caruso's "expressive gestures"; instead, he transformed his vocal performance into a style characterized by "classical harmonious order," which might perhaps have had a slightly vague or pale effect if it weren't for the overwhelming brilliance of his voice and the fantastic energy of his delivery.[3]

Two Italian tenors dominated the scene in the 1950s: Mario del Monaco (1915–82) and Giuseppe di Stefano (born in 1921). The former positively radiated the self-assurance, the energy, the macho bellicosity of a Roman tribune and sang with unflagging brilliance and therefore with all the more unbearable monotony. If one were ever to extol the glories of concrete, then most appropriately with the voice of del Monaco, who feared absolutely nothing on earth, with the possible exception of the *piano*. The Sicilian Giuseppe di Stefano had the temperament of a Latin lover and the suggestive charlatanism of a pizza vendor, coupled with a dazzlingly beautiful and shamelessly exploited but always overtaxed voice. He outsang himself to such an extent that his high notes already sounded as rough as sandpaper early in his career. He was the one who cautioned Pavarotti about the mistakes of his youth—and they were not only those of a musician, but those of a gambler, a daredevil, as well.

But who, when talking about the opera of the 1950s, still speaks of Mario del Monaco or Giuseppe di Stefano? Who still speaks of Carlo Bergonzi, whose vocal abilities were not as effective or penetrating, but who did have more stylistic skill? Who talks about Alfredo Kraus, whose youthful and vibrant singing belies his sixty-plus years? Or about the chameleonlike, stylistically confident and adaptable Nicolai Gedda? Who, finally, still remembers Giuseppe Campora, Gianni Poggi, Ferrucio Tagliavini, Giacinto Prandelli, Gianfranco Cecchele, Flaviano Labò, or even the brilliant Gianni Raimondi?[4] Who even mentions *tenorini* like Luigi Alva, Nicola Monti, Ugo Benelli, *et tutti quanti* when the conversation turns away from the art of singing or focuses on theatrical talent?

A NEW BEGINNING
IN THE PAST

If we listen again today to the recording of virtually any of the best-known tenors, baritones, and basses during this period, we have a distinct feeling of a decline of male vocalism to extremely low levels: lack of technical support, and hence forced and uneven production; no runs or messa di voce; *inability to sing legato and to bring the tone down to* piano *and* pianissimo; *high notes either throaty or lacking in ring or strident or shouted. . . . The cleaning-up operation begun by singers like Corelli, Bergonzi, McNeil, and continued by Kraus, Pavarotti, Bruson, on the other hand, was carried out on a repertoire generally alien to that of authentic bel canto; and when the seeds sown by Callas brought to the forefront Joan Sutherland and Marilyn Horne, a situation was created . . . to which virtually all of us today are accustomed and resigned: the tremendous disparity in technical, stylistic, and expressive level between these two extraordinary virtuoso artists and the tenors, baritones, and basses who sang side by side with them in Baroque opera and the operas of Rossini.*

RODOLFO CELLETTI, *A History of Bel Canto*

{ 8 7 }

*C*ould it be that the Caruso myth was betrayed, dissolved, or buried when or because Hollywood tried to revive it with that fine fellow who slicked his hair down and had such a radiantly naive laugh? When an artist was transformed into a "this way to the gondola" tourist guide? At least that matches the common (and less than common) man's dreams of a brilliant career. Italian mothers no longer place all their hopes in golden throats, "but rather in the bosoms and backsides of their growing daughters, in dreams of a movie career."[1]

Mario del Monaco and Giuseppe di Stefano undoubtedly achieved a certain fame, but the myth of the tenor was suspended for a time; the only singer who made it to the heights of stardom was a young girl from the Bronx called Maria Callas. She was the one who saved the operatic stage from simpering souls and *femmes fragiles,* from peasant wenches, hawking fishwives, and petit bourgeois coquettes. It was she and she alone who used her "stylized vocal delirium" (Fontana) to portray long-suffering, revengeful, and alienated women, and to enter into the realm of their insanity. This realm also happened to be the mad world of sexual desires, dreams, and jealousies, and Callas made it accessible to all—and in the 1950s no less, an era of dull conformity and weary morality. By exposing the public to the deep underlying layers of the psyche in her own irritating way, Callas was more than a sensation, she was a scandal. Yet when she sang the role of Norma next to the Pollione of such

singers as Mario Filippeschi, Mario del Monaco, and Franco
Corelli, who no longer radiated even a hint of charming,
aristocratic elegance; when she sang the role of Lucia next to
street Romeos (Giuseppe di Stefano, Giuseppe Campora)
without the grace of romantic youth; when she sang Gilda
next to Casanovas of the beer hall, or Amina together with
anemic *Magic Mountain* waifs (Cesare Valletti not included),[2] or Elvira paired with playboy aristocrats—in a
word: when Maria Callas made the music of romantic Italian
opera, the late heyday of *canto fiorito,* come alive in her own
inimitable manner, all she found was earnestly willing or
competent but hardly congenial tenor partners. She found no
rococo virtuoso along the lines of Fernando de Lucia as
partner to her Rosina, her Fiorilla, her Armida, no romantically youthful hero like the young Lauri-Volpi for her
Norma, her Elvira or Lucia, no graceful charmer for her
Amina like Tito Schipa or de Lucia.

   To put it yet another way, this time in terms contrary to
fact: Luciano Pavarotti could have become this tenor, for he
has the voice, the temperament, and the eclectic disposition
that says with Molière, "Je prends mon bien où je le trouve."
Let's indulge ourselves for a moment and allow this specula-
tion, this suspension of historical fact. Let's assume that that
star called Maria Callas had not wandered into the alien
universe we call the opera business. Let's assume that she
hadn't set those deep underlying layers of the psyche free
among the public and with them an interest in love-starved

and blissfully suffering women who turn into existential out-
siders because of their extreme emotions. The repertoire
would be impoverished—all the Joan Sutherlands, Montserrat Caballés, and Beverly Sillses, the Teresa Berganzas and
Marilyn Hornes, would never have passed through the por-
tals into what Caballé has called the *terra incognita* of romantic opera.

Furthermore, to continue our reverie, only Radames and
Manrico, Andrea Chenier and Canio, Rodolfo and Calaf
would have been obligatory for tenors—in other words, the
roles made famous by del Monaco and Richard Tucker, Jussi
Björling and Franco Corelli. But that would also have been
a kind of singing that had exhausted itself in imitating
Caruso, exhausted itself to the point of absurdity. To pursue
this train of thought even further: with all due reserve regarding del Monaco, for I respect his portrayals of Alvaro (especially on the live recording under Dimitri Mitropoulos), of
Andrea Chenier, of Canio, and of Otello as being evocative
and to some extent dramatically riveting, my memory—and
the ear possesses a power of recall all its own—fails to deliver
another unmistakably unique portrayal that might match
Callas's rendition of Norma, Violetta, or Tosca.[3]

After a decade of aesthetic leveling (or even trivialization),
the 1960s took a turn in reaction to the revolution unleashed
by Maria Callas. As one critic described it, it was a search for
the New among the Old. The moving force behind this
search was the Australian soprano Joan Sutherland, who

sang the role of Clotilda next to Callas's Norma in the latter's London debut in 1952. Sutherland would surely have grown into the specialized field of *lirico spinto* had she not perceived her own truly unique opportunities in the effect that Callas produced: Sutherland realized she could pursue an archival approach to bel canto. And it's no accident that such interpreters as Nikolaus Harnoncourt were beginning to show an interest in historical performance practices at the same time, not least among which was the art of florid singing.

The word *archival* is not meant in any derogatory sense, but simply to distinguish this historical approach from that of a realistic one. By employing her exceptional dramatic and theatrical talents, the great Callas had not only revived a repertoire that had been in a state of suspended animation for the previous four decades, but also used it to expose "deep layers" and thus to let something of the utopian potential in works such as *Norma* and *Medea*, *La Sonnambula* and *Lucia di Lammermoor* shine through. Yet there had never been moments of self-sufficiency in her singing, moments of self-fulfilling and narcissistic virtuosity. Sutherland introduced something different. She, who had initially sung lyric and youthful dramatic roles in the 1950s and found herself on the road to becoming a *soprano spinto*, developed into a *virtuosa* under the guidance of her husband, Richard Bonynge, and encouraged by the renaissance of romantic Italian opera initiated by Maria Callas. In Pavarotti's view, Sutherland, who in the early 1990s ended an almost forty-year career, was the "most perfect singer as far as technique is concerned that this century has known."4 In his recollections of Rubini, Chorley wrote that this particular tenor took obvious pleasure in his own singing and that this feeling couldn't help but communicate itself to the public. The same holds true of the radiance that emanated from Sutherland; she was not, like Callas, a tragedian, a Dusa *reincarnata*, but rather a nightingale, a creature of nature—but one with a sublime artistic nature. In Stendhal's terms, Sutherland's singing could touch the deepest recesses of the human soul and do so by means of the pure and unclouded beauty that lies at the very heart of cantabile. Her singing didn't emerge as the expression of an emotion, nor as the trembling confessions of an overflowing or, as was the case with Callas, of a tortured soul, but rather as an elegy.

WHAT YOU INHERITED FROM
YOUR FATHERS

*With the romantic opera, especially with Bellini and Don-
izetti, the tenor has finally acquired a status equal to that
of the great women's roles. Yet his voice must first go
through a stylizing process; it has to be soft and lovely and
capable of a* pianissimo *swathed in the glow of the moon;
it has to evoke infinite distances and the shimmer of star-
studded heavens. The tenor must also integrate several of
the vocal features of the castrati. He will sing up to G with
the chest voice, but will reach the high notes . . . with the*
falsettone *or the head voice . . . and with almost feminine
sounds. To hear a voice that could enchant audiences in days
gone by, and us today, one need only listen to Luciano
Pavarotti's recording of* I Puritani. *Swept along by the
Australian soprano Joan Sutherland, one of the great vocalists and archaeologists of song, Pavarotti draws a marvelous melodic bow in the sky during the opera's finale,
"Ell'è tremante / Ell'è spirante," an arc that climbs higher
and higher until, with a peak falsetto F, it loses all characteristics of earthly gender and turns into a pure and abstract
incarnation of the pangs of love. When the first great tenor
star, Giovanni Battista Rubini, sang this piece, not only*

Heinrich Heine but also Count Metternich were moved
to tears. Such are the strange harmonics of taste.

LUCA FONTANA, "Che bella voce"

*W*ilfrid Mellers has observed that, like so many other
things in our society, musical interpretation is dependent on the spirit of the times, on political as well as
aesthetic trends, and not lastly, on fads.[1] This is just as true
for singing. The pathos of so-called court opera was superseded by the melodic line of the new objectivity. A short time
later, say, with Benjamino Gigli or Helge Roswaenge, the
rhetorical excesses of the political speech infiltrated the vocalist's performance, and even as eminent a singer as Richard
Tauber sweetened Lehár's *amoretti* with sentimental kitsch.
And the vocal gesticulations of Caruso, imitated for decades
by just about every tenor after him, were resurrected yet again
by Mario Lanza before finally being abandoned to ridicule.

In 1960 Joan Sutherland and Richard Bonynge released an
album on Decca called *The Age of Bel Canto* in collaboration
with Marilyn Horne and Richard Conrad. This anthology,
like a second one that Horne released on Decca featuring a
Malibran-Viardot program, was distinguished by a higher
ambition than that of merely presenting brilliant vocal ef-

fects. It was an attempt at a systematic reconstruction of the techniques constituting the formal language of bel canto. Unfortunately, Richard Conrad was no more than a *tenorino* as far as his vocal abilities were concerned. At most, his voice could carry a romantic ballad or an elegaic cantabile. Despite all his polish, Conrad would have been hard pressed to revitalize the role of the romantic *primo uomo* onstage. Such a task called for a full-blooded tenor capable of producing the vigorous tones that the public had come to expect since the days of Duprez, Tamberlik, and Caruso, without the crude and by now worn-out effects that Giuseppe di Stefano, Mario del Monaco, and Richard Tucker thought absolutely indispensible. It also needed a tenor who, unlike the brilliant Swede Jussi Björling or his cool and collected countryman Nicolai Gedda, would exude the aura of a crooning eroticon, a singing sex symbol.

The romantic repertoire that Maria Callas resuscitated was subjected to a complete renovation. It was no longer enough to feature but one single star in the romantic, tender, elegaic roles, as had been the case in the 1950s. Decca recorded Mario del Monaco not only as Radames, Otello, Canio, and Chenier, but as the Duke and Pollione as well—although other interpreters technically and stylistically more suitable were certainly available. RCA did the same thing: they engaged Richard Tucker for roles—the Duke, Edgardo—that would have been more appropriate for the young Ferruccio Tagliavini, with his honey-sweet voice that positively oozed *morbidezza.* The result of these practices was that the per-formance of parts that ought to have been sung lightly and elegantly turned into an al fresco image, as it were, all because the industry insisted upon adhering to a rigid and outdated tradition. Jan Peerce, Mario del Monaco, and Giuseppe di Stefano, limited as he was in the higher ranges, sang the Duke; di Stefano, Edgardo and Arturo; del Monaco, Mario Filippeschi, and Franco Corelli all sang Pollione. The mere fullness of the voice was more highly regarded than any artis-tic finesse. From a subjective point of view it is perhaps un-derstandable (although regrettable) that singers with the lighter voices thought they could compete with these heavy-weights. As Irving Kolodin points out in his *Story of the Metropolitan Opera*, this is particularly true for Ferruccio Tagliavini;[2] and it can be said to apply to Giuseppe di Stefano as well. As his recordings of the late 1940s show, di Stefano was a lyric tenor with a velvety smooth voice. He was already ignoring the rules of the "ceiling" early on in his career, how-ever, by forcing the chest voice into the higher ranges and thereby losing his full upper register. Both tenors not only risked singing parts that were too difficult for them but also lent the lyric parts too much tonal weight.

When Pavarotti first met Joan Sutherland and Richard Bonynge, the tenor was not yet a star, which means he was still in his formative stage. Following his debut on April 29, 1961, in Reggio nell'Emilia, Pavarotti filled his whole first season with only two roles, those of the Duke and Alfredo, and in a total of only sixteen performances at that. During the 1962–63 season he added only two more to his repertoire: Edgardo and Pinkerton. That year he appeared in thirty-four performances. The following season brought forty-two performances and a single new role, that of Idamante in Mozart's *Idomeneo*, which he then sang twelve times at the Glyndebourne Festival. Pavarotti sang his first opera with Joan Sutherland on February 15, 1965, in Miami and Fort Lauderdale. Beginning May 26 there followed five performances of Vincenzo Bellini's *La Sonnambula* at Covent Garden, and immediately thereafter the Sutherland-Williamson International Grand Opera Company—which counted Elizabeth Harwood and Spiro Malas among its members—traveled to Australia. Pavarotti sang Nemorino, Elvino, Edgardo, and Alfredo.

Richard Bonynge recalled that in those days Pavarotti was a *tenore di grazia* with an above-average volume and a strong projection. Perhaps this is as good a place as any to explain the various distinctions among tenor voices as a supplement to the history or genealogy of the tenor, which has so far neglected the florid repertoire of the eighteenth century. The lightweight among tenors is the *leggiero* or *di grazia*, the one Rossini used in his Neapolitan operas. Lindoro or Almaviva have to sing coloratura and thus can't afford to shy away from the climb to the highest regions. Voices of greater weight are called for in *Armida*, *Le Siège de Corinth*, *Semiramide*, and above all in *Guillaume Tell*, but not to such an extent that the tessitura would have been lower. Today's audience would presumably be irritated if the *acuti*—C, C sharp, and D— were to sound as they did when Nourrit or Rubini sang them, which is to say, with the *voix mixte* or *voce mista*, an art most perfected among postwar tenors by Nicolai Gedda.3 Genuine coloraturas are not produced by wobbling about or sliding through the musical runs, as one so frequently hears, and even the aspiration of vowels—the insertion of a voice-less aspirant *h*—borders on the intolerable.4 Coloratura is not supposed to be treated like a burdensome appendix to the musical phrase; it has to unfold like a vocal gesture and be transformed into expression.

Expression—a vague word and an unfortunate one, as well. Its meaning can't be reduced to the articulation of a mighty affect, to the agitated imitation of sobbing hysterics in veris-tic operas whose tenors shriek out their *aria d'urlo*.5 Strange as it may seem, what counts as expression is not created when a singer employs the identical affect in every role of every single composer, even if these gestures are meant or even felt to be ever so genuine. Good intentions have always been the opposite of art, and feeling belongs in the stuffy sphere of sentiment. Expression lies first and foremost in an "analyti-cal, richly nuanced . . . phrasing" (Rodolfo Celletti), which is to say, in the precise formation of each vocal technique, be it ever so small or unprepossessing. The sum of the techniques at one's disposal produces form (in the sense of a vocal grammar), and only after such a grammar is mastered can a

singer advance to a higher level and imbue the mechanics of
singing with the colors of expression or emotion.

The essence of coloratura in Rossini or of ornamentation
in Bellini—and especially the suspensions or *gruppetti*—is
thus much more than mere decoration. Such embellishments, or to borrow a phrase from Carl Dahlhaus, "veiling"
techniques, are an essential component of this type of music.
The incorporation of these arabesques and ornaments is still
being misinterpreted, even today, as the "vanity of prima
donnas," the "arbitrary willfulness of singers," or as "empty
virtuosity,"[6] but if one robs this type of music of these characteristic elements, the distortion would be no different than if
one were to enclose a rococo painting in a sleek art deco
frame. There is no way to perform these frills if the voice is
not flexible and completely controlled. It would be absurd to
demand from a voluminous, heavy voice such as that of
Lauritz Melchior or Mario del Monaco the same *agilità* as
one can from a light tenor along the lines of Luigi Alva or
Francisco Araiza. Even so, this doesn't exempt the singers of
the heavier mode from working, let's say, on sliding skills. On
the contrary, it is precisely "for the clumsier or the heavier
voices that tend toward oversupport that work on coloratura
is absolutely mandatory" (Martienßen-Lohmann), in much
the same way that mobility and speed are absolute prereq-
uisites for a weight lifter, for example, in order to help him
find his rhythm. Rhythm alone is what lends tension and
excitement to coloratura singing.

Rossini's coloratura parts and the lighter roles in Bellini's works are always sung by very light tenors, at least on the recorded versions. As far as "decoration" is concerned, these florid elements are always sung like études. The undeniably competent Luigi Alva sang parts like Almaviva in *Il Barbiere di Siviglia* or Don Ramiro in *La Cenerentola* the way a well-trained piano student plays an exercise by Czerny. To blame this on a lack of vocal ability alone is out of line here, for it's much more the consequence of the singer's total submission to the "dictatorship of the baton" that Verdi so deplored, a dictatorship that prohibits any creative vocal play, which is to say, the improvisation we admire on the recordings of Fernando de Lucia, for example. All the more deplorable is that this eventual impoverishment of the score is done in the name of so-called fidelity to the work.

On the other hand, to deplore the absence of Fernando de Lucia today is to fail to appreciate another fact: namely, that the true rulers of the opera business, the conductors ranging from Arturo Toscanini and Herbert von Karajan all the way up to Sir Georg Solti, Claudio Abbado, and Riccardo Muti, have managed to expatriate, as it were, this type of singer for the last eight decades. For most of them, the music of Rossini, Bellini, and Donizetti was a *quantité négligeable* anyway, and when a conductor such as Claudio Abbado came to terms with Rossini or Ricardo Muti with Donizetti's *Don Pasquale*, it was mainly a matter of the rhythmic dynamics of the performance and rarely one of vocal nuancing. There are

no more de Lucias because there shouldn't be, there can't
be; we simply don't have a robust tenor like Hermann Jadlowker, who could sing the coloraturas in "Fuor del mar"
from Mozart's *Idomeneo* or in "Ecco ridente in cielo" from
Rossini's *Barbiere* with full, immaculately rounded coloratura
tones. Francisco Araiza, gifted not only with a voluminous
lyric voice but with verve and a rhythmic sense of movement
as well, yielded to the bad habit of singing the stylistically as
well as otherwise controversial "hahaha," or laughing, coloratura. Always supposing he had a certain degree of sliding
skill, today's *tenore leggiero* would probably be cast in the
following roles: Don Ottavio in Mozart's *Don Giovanni* and
Belmonte in *Die Entführung aus dem Serail*, Almaviva in
Barbiere, Don Ramiro in *La Cenerentola*, Lindoro in
L'Italiana in Algeri, Don Narciso in *Il Turco in Italia*, Ernesto
in *Don Pasquale*, Nemorino in *L'Elisir d'Amore*, Elvino in *La
Sonnambula*. In addition, he might be given light, high parts
like that of the fisherman in *Guillaume Tell* or Beppe in
Pagliacci.

The lyric tenor, particularly the *lirico spinto*, needs a somewhat greater tonal weight and, perhaps most importantly,
greater brilliance and penetrative power in the middle register as well as in the transitional tones leading to the upper
register. The lyric tenor's roles include Pollione in *Norma*,
Arturo in *I Puritani*, Edgardo in *Lucia di Lammermoor*, Alfredo in *La Traviata*, the Duke in *Rigoletto*, Des Grieux in
Manon Lescaut, Rodolfo in *La Bohème*, Cavaradossi in *Tosca*,

Pinkerton in *Madama Butterfly*, and Faust and Romeo in the operas of Charles Gounod. However, since every voice is a law unto itself—perhaps the only rule on which all voice teachers agree—responsible casting demands the greatest care and attention. Parts like that of the Duke or Arturo require an ability to extend effortlessly into the higher ranges; the Puccini roles require a solid, robust middle register, and whoever strains this by forcing the high notes immediately produces tones that sound as rough as pumice, which is what Giuseppe di Stefano did right from the start of his career.

To the dramatic tenor, the Italian *spinto*, belong some of the early and all the later Verdi parts after Manrico: Enzo in *La Gioconda*, Andrea Chenier, Canio, Turriddu, Calaf, Samson in the opera by Camille Saint-Saëns, Eleazar in *La Juive*, and many verismo parts, as well as, naturally, most of the Wagner parts. Experience has shown that a well-schooled, experienced, and above all technically expert *lirico spinto* can expand his repertoire into the heroic field. One need only think of Jussi Björling as the most outstanding example.

The Singing Eroticon

The singer really still is a beating drum,

or rather, a harp that plays its own music.

Here—in contrast to those previous remnants which

were rarely found and faintly bizarre, though important—

the music note has a definite site, namely a body that sings in

the process of acting. Here music, in the process of floating,

alights on a visible instrumental provenance. . . . What

has replaced the archaic magic of the object, to some

extent at least, is a kind of intrinsic magic of

the material, the singing love-poetry or the

instrumental live impetus of an especially

effusive display of the material

itself, which is localized.

ERNST BLOCH, *"Magic Rattle and Human Harp," in* Essays
on the Philosophy of Music

THE GREAT TRADITION

To sing mere sounds is a senseless performance no matter how much those sounds tickle the ears of the dear public, no matter how large the price paid the singer for their utterance. And it is the artist who must educate the public. . . . Patience, devotion, sincerity: these must be the watchwords of the student of singing.

WILLIAM JAMES HENDERSON, *The Art of Singing*

*T*he family tree of tenors and the genealogy of the various disciplines document the intimate connection between composition and performance. Rossini, Bellini, Donizetti, Verdi, Puccini, all wrote for the singers of their day, and these singers in turn sang mostly contemporary music. A concept such as repertoire or even masterwork presupposes a temporal distance, just as the mastering of the repertoire presupposes a specific attitude. This attitude is best described in terms of service or submission on the part of the artist. The guiding principle of the one who serves is an alleged "fidelity to the work," a slavish commitment to the printed notes of the score. As one of the first influential conductors of opera, Arturo Toscanini canonized this attitude, with the result that singers were forbidden the previously accepted and commonly practiced deviations from the printed score, deviations that served the spirit rather than the letter of the piece.

Toscanini has frequently been reproached for having leveled and partially destroyed the art of singing as well as the possibility of idiosyncratic diversions from the norm. This reproach has ricocheted off the aura that has come to surround his authority.[1] While his manner of perfecting the orchestral machine for the sake of improving its function is commonly accepted, vocal virtuosity and perfection are perceived as an expression of vanity. Orchestras such as the Chicago Symphony and the Berlin Philharmonic, led by *fortissimo* fanatics like Sir Georg Solti or Riccardo Muti, are watched and admired when they produce "orchestral strokes of crushing impact."[2] On the other hand, a singer who is able to project—to use the jargon—is considered ostentatious. When an Itzhak Perlman plays his *staccati* or *spiccati*, when a Horowitz thunders his octaves, the string- and keyboard-crazed reviewers delight in their transcendental virtuosity; when these same talents are displayed by Joan Sutherland, they are deprecatingly described as "showing off."[3]

It is not only because of this kind of aesthetic prejudice that singers are having a hard time in today's opera world, for like it or not, that world has entered the age of operatic *post-histoire* while still featuring the repertoire of more than three and a half centuries of musical tradition. Even though international stages rarely offer more than 120 to 150 works a year, and even though the repertoire rests on only a very few pillars bearing such names as Mozart, Wagner, Verdi, Puccini, and Strauss, the musicians of our day have long since led a second, technical existence: namely, as artist-interpreters for recording studios. Because the traditional repertoire has been exhausted by dozens, indeed hundreds of repeats and reissues, the recording industry now needs new works, which they invariably find among the existing stock. That is why it also needs specialized interpreters whose artistic talents justify the excavation.

It was for this if for no other reason that the music world turned to a revival of the so-called bel canto, an art form that was already on its deathbed the day it got its name, which is to say, toward the end of the nineteenth century.

We can dispense with a detailed historical digression here and focus instead on this particular vocal art, which was coarsened and corrupted during the period between 1910 and 1950. There are four fundamental technical abilities that are absolutely essential for the bel canto singer in order to fulfill certain stylistic requirements posed by the vocal music of the last three centuries. These include a clear, finely produced, and steady tone; a smooth legato; effortless dynamic control; and flexibility and agility in the execution of florid passages.[4] To repeat, these technical abilities are not an end in themselves, but the means by which musical expression is attained. And this expression, once again, is neither naturalistic nor realistic, but a purely aesthetic, artistic sound.

The finely produced, melodious tone is sustained, swelled, or retracted by means of the art of *messa di voce*, which is an expression of beauty in and of itself. This, however, brings us into the realm of the individual application of technique. It is the sound that moves or delights the soul. In bel canto the legato line is not only molded by a rhythmic fluidity more effective than a quick metric pulse; it also receives its tension by means of the "sculpting curve" of portamento. This in turn has nothing to do with an unsteady upward gliding of the note, which is the inevitable result of an unsure attack. The musical phrase is sensually as well as intellectually shaped by dynamic nuances, and these are what make the phrase "three-dimensional,"[5] as it were, and thus more expressive than if it were determined by rhythm and pitch alone. Finally, ornaments, fluently executed and woven into the total tension of the phrase, give it as well as the sense of the text its final polish. Only when the singer uses his voice as an instrument, only when it can reach out into every register, effortlessly and on command, and can do so in any tempo and with whatever volume is required—only then does singing become art.

Let's define our terms a bit more precisely. What do we mean by a "clean and steady tone"? A note that floats calmly and securely on the breath, is released without an audible click (glottal stop) of the vocal chords, is formed without an unwanted gasp of air (usually called breathiness), ends without a thrust of residual air, is "struck" cleanly in every register, or, if it's supposed to be expressive, is "attacked" and never impaired by what is called tremolo or wobble. Such a tone is intensified the same way a note on a violin is, by means of a quick, controlled, and precisely timed vibrato of measured amplitude. This mastery of tone is the absolute and indispensible prerequisite for the legato line, the smooth transition of tone from syllable to syllable. This transition has to occur without releases, without extraneous noises, without gasps of breath prior to a change of position or a shift between registers. And it can never allow any hesitation before articulating the more difficult consonants or before forming the more difficult vowels. The aspiration of an initial vowel by inserting an unvoiced *h* is considered a cardinal sin; this hissing sound would tear a hole, as it were, into the fabric of the line. The tone is carried along by a portamento, which in the original sense means to carry the voice on the breath.

Without the third technical element, dynamic and rhythmic flexibility, the vocal music of the eighteenth and especially that of the nineteenth century is neither technically nor expressively performable. Whereas in Mozart's music the dynamic scale is still relatively narrow, Verdi and Wagner, say, and surely the verists rely on strong, often upon the most impetuous, dynamic contrasts. The trend toward an *expression outrée* could already be found in the work of the later

Rossini—in his *Armida*, for instance—and was further developed in Italian romantic opera. Operagoers have long since become accustomed to the fact that the so-called Verdi and Puccini singers (Martinelli, Pertile, Merli, del Monaco, Tucker, Crelli, Domingo, to name only the tenors) ignore the *piano* indications especially, but not exclusively, in the high tessitura. Those conductors committed to fidelity to the work, be they known by the names of Toscanini, Karajan, Solti, Muti, or Abbado, have accepted this state of affairs if for no other reason than that one has to sing loudly in order to be heard above the (too loud) orchestra, or because they simply accept the fact that singers are no longer able to sing softly. The word *softly* here—and, again, this refers to the tone itself—does not mean a diminished and dully aspirated *mezzo forte*, but an active, vital, pulsating, sonorously transporting tone like those produced by Joan Sutherland, Marilyn Horne, or Nicolai Gedda. If one listens to the recordings of the very young Caruso (pre-1906) or to those of Mattia Battistini and Fernando de Lucia, one can experience the musical and expressive sense of fine and dynamic singing. Today this type of *piano* singing has been relegated to the domain of a few lieder singers, led by such artists as Dietrich Fischer-Dieskau, Janet Baker, and Peter Pears.

There remains the fourth essential element of the art of singing: agility (*agilità*) or the flexibility of the voice. For years this skill had been not only forgotten but just about condemned as well. The ornamented repertoire disappeared from the stages for a long time, and lost with it was the specific technique necessary to produce the effect. This was especially true among male singers. Many interpreters of Rossini's Almaviva in *Il Barbiere di Siviglia* captured on postwar recordings get caught up in the *fioritura* like flies in a spider's web. In an article on Fernando de Lucia and Mattia Battistini, the "twin glories" of the Italian opera at the turn of the century, Will Crutchfield writes that on the Callas recording Luigi Alva jabbered and cheated his way through the coloratura chains without clearly articulating the individual notes, while under the perfectionist Abbado he "had to insert hundreds of little 'h's' to get him through."[6] Francisco Araiza employs similarly dirty tricks. Yet it must be said that the many Rossini performances of the past ten to fifteen years have improved the situation: there hasn't been a bass as agile as Samuel Ramey for decades. Even so, there still remains a lacuna. As mentioned above, it's again a matter of the quality of the vocal tones, of the musically expressive animation of vocal gestures.

With this exposition on matters technical, Pavarotti's course as a singer has come into full view, even if it hasn't been discussed specifically. He, the *tenore di grazia* possessing significant volume and projection, began by singing the lyric and *spinto* roles of Puccini and Verdi. By doing so he proved a perfect match for the practical qualifications theater was demanding during the early 1960s. The romantic repertoire that Callas so brilliantly mastered was no longer the focus of attention; on the contrary, the many revivals featuring Montserrat Caballé, Beverly Sills, Renata Scotto, and Joan Sutherland were long looked upon as self-glorifications of "vain" divas, and recourse to the formal language of bel canto was met with a downright irrelevant, historically false critique if not bitter polemic, especially in Germany.7 What Rodolfo Celletti points out bears repeating here: Maria Callas was initially responsible only for a revival of dramatic coloratura singing, but it turned out to be irresistible simply because it was so general. According to Celletti, it was only through the efforts of Sutherland and Horne that "pure virtuosity, elegance of execution, respect for laws obligatory for the pre-Verdi repertoire, such as improvisation of semi-cadenzas and cadenzas and da capo variations" were once again brought to the public's attention.8

As mentioned above, the "Sutherland connection" was to prove pivotal for Pavarotti. The responsible agent was Joan Ingpen, who headed the casting office of the Royal Opera at Covent Garden for the conductor Sir Georg Solti in the mid-1960s. She had engaged the young tenor toward the end of 1963 as an understudy for Giuseppe di Stefano, who was then feared to be unreliable. When he actually did perform in his stead, Pavarotti's career experienced the catapult so familiar to all. Nine months later in Glyndebourne (July 1964), he sang the part of Idamante in no fewer than twelve performances, but it was a part originally written for a castrato. As eager to learn as only young singers are, Pavarotti followed the advice of Jani Strasser, who was in charge of musical preparation in Glyndeborne, and he took pains to acquire a more delicately shaded dynamic accentuation and to learn the art of *piano* singing.⁹

Joan Ingpen tipped off Richard Bonynge, who then heard the tenor during one of his rehearsals in London. Four performances of *Lucia di Lammermoor* in the United States in February 1965 were followed three months later by the first systematic collaboration of the two singers in Bellini's *La Sonnambula* in Covent Garden. During the three months in Australia, with their thirty-nine performances, Pavarotti underwent, if not a complete retraining, at least a period of "learning by doing." Amazed, the tenor observed that the diva who had long been extolled as *la stupenda* was not only by far more technically skilled than he was, but more athletically fit as well. She sang her way through the role of Amina during a dress rehearsal in the afternoon and the role of Violetta in a performance that same evening without betraying the slightest sign of fatigue. "I saw that lady sing both in full voice," he recalls, "and at the end she was not tired." He himself, so he later confessed, couldn't always depend on his voice completely and had always accepted his teachers' suggestion that his insecurities might be due to fatigue. "What I learned from Joan was that when I felt tired it was because I did not control the diaphragm." Flashing that playfully mischievous smile that spices his anecdotes, Pavarotti related how he once told Bonynge during a rehearsal, "Excuse me,

but I am going to put my hand on your wife's stomach."
Whereupon his hand followed her abdominal muscles as she
sang and felt how they raised the diaphragm when she in-
haled.[10] That's how he learned how to sing on his breath, the
prerequisite for major parts of his later repertoire.

This skill simply can't be subsumed under the term *bel
canto*, as is almost always the case in this country. Pavarotti
had never risked the masterly demands of *canto fiorito*, thus
had never sung anything written between Handel and Rossini. In his case, the star in excelsis, public demand may have
been responsible: as Rossini's Count Almaviva at the Met,
even with the most glorious of masterly performances, he
would never have had as much success as he did with the
salvo of high C's that he shot off in "Ah, mes amis" from
Donizetti's *La Fille du Régiment*. His performance in Bellini's *I Puritani* as well as his recourse to the stratospheric
high notes of the adored Giovanni Battista Rubini served as
a peg for *Newsweek*'s first big story devoted entirely to him.

It's not entirely certain whether Pavarotti would have held
his own in the florid style, mainly because he hadn't had
enough practice. When confronted with its elements in his
role as Nemorino, for instance, in the coloratura cadenza of
"Una furtiva lagrima," or as Elvino during the florid passages
of "Prendi, l'anel ti dono," he handles the challenge by singing the running passages less fluently than Caruso, despite a
leaner tone. He produces the embellishments clearly enough,
but with what might be called a passive inflection, not a

particularly melodic *piano*. When he sings Handel's "Care selve" one also misses the impeccable octave leap to the high A's that one has come to admire in John McCormack's model interpretation. This may be due to his tendency to dam up his voice, with the result that the tone can't always sail along the breath.[11] More important to Pavarotti than the softly fluted tone of Gigli's *pianissimo*, more important too than the art of *messa di voce*, which can be learned with greater profit by studying Mattia Battistini than by studying Tito Schipa, was the transparent brilliance of his *acuti*. Or should we say that they were more important not *to* him but rather *for* him, precisely because that monster currently represented by conductors, impresarios, colleagues, and fans can only be assuaged with the fat, juicy morsels of high notes and nothing else?

Pavarotti is fully aware of the problem. Martin Mayer quotes him as saying that, as a tenor, one has good reasons to wish his predecessors such as Gilbert-Louis Duprez or Enrico Tamberlik to the devil, because they're the ones who created the unholy cult surrounding the high notes emanating from full cheeks. And he may be speaking out of bitter experience when he says that conductors disdain the virtuosity of *canto fiorito* and the audience no longer demands the art of *piano* singing.[12]

Is it bitter experience or self-knowledge that's almost always hidden behind these explanations and self-justifications? Even when his singing was stylistically cleaner and more differentiated than that of several of his colleagues of the 1950s, even when he was smart enough to avoid the difficult parts with which Giuseppi di Stefano sang himself out—despite all this, there can be no doubt that Pavarotti's ambition was always directed toward realizing the mythical role of the tenor. In all likelihood, all he wanted to be was the King of High C's.

And all his recordings show it—because his presence on record is greater than on stage. Unlike the singers of earlier times, he no longer works in an art world, which is a world unto itself, but as a guest star who turns up like a messiah, as it were, in guest appearances. He's no longer a singer in an artistic world that functions according to strict rules, but rather the cult figure of a faceless amusement industry; and there's no one who might be in the position to record his artistic development, his progress as well as his setbacks, his individuality, as could be done in the case of Caruso or even Maria Callas. Luciano Pavarotti leads a double life, and it's time to turn our attention to it.

PAVAROTTI ON RECORD

*With a bouquet of bel canto hits Luciano Pavarotti intro-
duces himself to the German record audience, and what a
program it is! He has combined a colorful palette of Italian
songs with his own musical talent, which immediately
identifies him as a tenor of the Neapolitan school. His
effortless execution of cantilenas, coloratura, and high notes
shows that this type of singing is, if possible, innate to him.
And what nature gave him he has polished to perfection
with the help of an extraordinary technique.*

BERND W. WESSLING's commentary on a
Pavarotti recital in 1968

No question about it—this is Pavarotti's Aïda. *It certainly
isn't anybody else's. The recording was made in Milan in
1985. . . . As ever the consistent artist, he sings here with his
usual beauty of tone and shapeliness of phrasing. "Celeste
Aïda" is effectively done at a flowing tempo, though it is a
shame the engineers felt impelled to help out the singer's
natural* diminuendo *on the B flat, making it sound as
though he is floating up into the rafters.*

From a review in *Opera*, July 1990

$\mathcal{T}$here are two ominous aspects of the recording industry: On the one hand, the record is a vehicle of shame-
less hype over which the artist has no control even though it
concerns him directly. On the other hand, it's also an instrument for the artificial amplification of the voice. The first of
the texts quoted above should never have found its way into
print, because it can only too easily be turned against the
young singer, and the B flat that was technically manipulated
in such an irritating way should never have found its way past
the studio door. And these are by no means the only absurdi-
ties to be found on the many, the unendingly many recordings Pavarotti has made.

True, a singer can record roles that exceed his vocal powers, but only to a certain extent. In the studio setting he can
distribute over a number of recording sessions whatever
difficulties he might not be able to master in the course of a
single evening. By the same token, no studio can turn a
tenorino into a Duke, a lyric tenor into Manrico, Chenier, or
Canio. Even so, as Lauri-Volpi, Jussi Björling, and Pavarotti
have all amply demonstrated, there surely are possibilities for
the *lirico spinto* to extend his innate talents without exceeding
the limits of his vocal powers. And if it's taken seriously as
an artistic medium, why shouldn't the record give the artist
a chance to present himself as completely as possible?

It goes without saying that the public as well as the critics
measure an artist against the expectations he raises via the
medium. Moreover, as Maria Callas and Walter Legge have

shown, it's precisely through and in combination with the technical and aesthetic potentials of a sound recording that the status and quality of an artist can be demonstrated. And this doesn't necessarily apply only to the choice of repertoire. The fact that a Caruso, a Richard Tauber, an Elisabeth Schwarzkopf have recorded Neapolitan songs, hit tunes, operatic arias, and even kitschy melodies doesn't compromise their status as artists. On the contrary, it's precisely in this kind of environment that one can study that very artistic interpretation and vocal refinement that Alfred Polgar had in mind when he said, "It's still an art, even though it isn't art."

Some of the albums featuring the younger Pavarotti are delightful, including one he cut in the second year of his recording career. It presents Gaetano Donizetti's *La Fille du Régiment* with Joan Sutherland under the direction of Richard Bonynge. John Steane writes about it in his book *The Grand Tradition*: "One of the best performances by any tenor on record, his Tonio has the character and polish of a much older singer, while his voice is that of a young man and in absolutely prime condition. The solo 'Ah, mes amis, quel jour de fête' is the kind of *tour de force* which, recorded sixty years earlier, would be the classic collector's piece; perhaps Escalaïs compares in combining such brilliance of high notes and energy along with a musical imagination. The leaps to high C are tireless, and are not there as a great show-off but as part of the fun of the fête, expressions of joy and energy like a youngster doing cartwheels or standing on his head, and none the less artistic for that."[1]

The recording session took place shortly after the London performance of the work, and it was this performance to which Pavarotti owed his unprecedented success in the United States. Moreover, it was in this part that he toured the United States as a member of the Met Ensemble—and the fact that the Spanish tenor Alfredo Kraus also sang the role in 1986 speaks for itself. His performance was recorded live and shows that time does not necessarily have to take its toll on the voice: at the time of his recording, Kraus was fifty years old.

THE KING OF HIGH C'S

*Yeah, he sings all the C's, but who cares? They're the
size of a pea.*

CONRAD L. OSBORNE

Let's leave Steane's homage to the voice for a moment
and turn to two of Pavarotti's early recitals, one in 1968
and the other in 1969-70, to see how he sounded back then.
We'll use as our standard the technical principles discussed
in the previous section. Because of the emphasis on mistakes
and weaknesses, what follows may seem to be excessively
critical, but it is not meant to be so by any means.

In their day, these recitals were looked upon, and surely
rightly so, as unusual talent tests. They're all the more interesting in retrospect, especially since Pavarotti has yet to
surpass the quality of those performances in many respects.
In those days one was most impressed by the sound of his
pure tenor voice and of its radiant pitch, with the metallic
quality Italians call *squillo*; impressive too was the quality of
the timbre and the singer's impeccable diction. Even today,

Pavarotti sings with a genuine vowel coloration and carefully formed consonants, and still commands a good sense of rhythm with an occasional tendency to fade in.

Strangely enough, taking part in both of these recitals were the Vienna Opera Orchestra and the New Philharmonia Orchestra under the direction of Leone Magiera, Nicola Rescigno, and Ewald Downes, all apparently brought together merely for the purpose of the recording. On the first disc—the one Wessling praised so fatuously—Pavarotti sings arias by Donizetti and Verdi. None of them make significant demands on the vocalist's *agilità*, nor does he have to sing any coloratura or even a fairly complicated *fioritura*. It's therefore perfectly appropriate to wonder whether he could have sung a florid passage at all, given the tone production he employs here. As far as the sound of his singing is concerned, in this recital Pavarotti relied on a narrowly focused and metallically compressed tone produced under great pressure, a tone that didn't rest on the breath and allowed as few dynamic nuances as it did colorful shadings. This is unfortunate, for he was obviously trying to do just that, as witnessed by his recitative of Fernando's aria from *La Favorita*. The *piano* tones slide back into the body, as it were, as a consequence of the strongly constricted passages marking the end of a phrase. In other words, the *piano* is passive and dull, possessing neither shine nor luster. Moreover, the overall impression suffers from the singer's tendency to produce explosive initial sounds and accents, as well as from the shocklike expulsions of breath at the end of phrases, and sometimes also from a garish fading-in of vowels. Relatively rare are the portamenti characteristic of the frozen movement of a sculpture. This is particularly evident in Fernando's "Spirto Gentil." Where Caruso sings two phrases with one breath and lets the tone, which is finely modulated and rhythmically varied, sail along on one stream of air, Pavarotti presses the phrase out like toothpaste from a tube. The high C in the second stanza isn't lifted the way Caruso sang it; instead, Pavarotti scoops up to it—a procedure that has absolutely nothing to do with the portamento of the breath.

If the Donizetti pieces lack the elegance of the romantic tenor, then the excerpts from the Verdi operas lack all delicacy of phrasing. This, too, is a function of the braced quality of the singing, which leads to horrible mistakes in intonation in one or two short a cappella phrases in Rodolfo's recitative to the aria from *Luisa Miller*. To be fair, Pavarotti omits the overused *espressivo* frills that several tenors from the 1930s to the 1950s used to insert, but in his rendition of Riccardo's aria from *Un Ballo in Maschera* his cantabile has virtually no dynamic nuance except in the middle register. On the whole, his cantabile remains two-dimensional, defined solely through the pitch and the relatively inflexible rhythm. It's difficult to say whether it would have been sung any better or any differently under a more flexible conductor, but one thing is sure: it certainly would have, had a Tullio Serafin been on the podium and a Walter Legge in the control room. Disappointing too is the creative aspect of the theatrical presentation, for more imagination here would have produced more evocative vocal gestures. "O figli, o figli miei" at the beginning of MacDuff's aria in Verdi's *Macbeth* is no rhetorical exclamation—it's a scream, a cry of pain. Pavarotti fails most miserably in lending this moment its appropriate expression, although he does shade the following cantilena with a suprising degree of emotion.

That he was capable of much more expressive phrasing is shown by the second recital, especially since Nicola Rescigno was on the stand. This time Pavarotti sings the recitative "Non mi lasciare" to "O muto asil" from *Guglielmo Tell*, the aria "Ah, sì, ben mio" from *Il Trovatore*, and above all "Cielo e mar" with youthful enthusiasm, expansive phrasing, and unusually delicate dynamic nuances combined with a lean delivery, even if he does lack a truly glowing *piano dolce*. In "Ah, sì, ben mio" he actually produces the trill, but it lacks the polish of a completely controlled oscillation and fails to capture the noble and elegaic pathos of the song. In this respect Björling is head and shoulders above him. Nevertheless, most people will listen (or will have listened) to this program less for its vocal finesses than for its display of high notes. At the end of the "Corriam" *stretta* from Rossini's *Tell* Pavarotti holds his high C for a full twelve seconds, at the end of "Di quella pira" from Verdi's *Il Trovatore* no less than thirteen. In "A te, o cara" from Bellini's *I Puritani* he actually reaches the C sharp (D flat). Yet these *acuti*, extremely strained and not only compressed but narrow and colorless, have a synthetic sound and give the impression that Pavarotti was hopelessly out of his depth in those days singing roles like that of Arnoldo and Manrico. He has much more trouble with the fifth jump from "asil" to "pianto," for example, than did the old and ailing Francesco Tamagno so long ago, and even when compared to the sovereign, mighty Giovanni Martinelli the younger singer didn't cut all that good a figure. He would have tackled the music of Arturo, which is a perfect fit for the tenor range, better if he had used a gentler projection. The romance, once sung by Giacomo Lauri-Volpi (on a 1928 recording) with noble pathos and iridescent intonation, loses all its magic as a result of the permanent strain and the attempt to achieve a metallic brilliance. The serenade "Come è gentil" is a total failure: one gets the impression that Pavarotti is trying to wake the dead. He proves to be a bit more elegant in his rendition of Rodolfo's "Che gelida manina," even if he is still nowhere near as lively and imaginative as he was under Herbert von Karajan in the later complete recording, and Federico's *lamento* from Francesco Cilèa's *L'Arlesiana* is one of the best cuts on the whole disc.

The recording of Donizetti's comic opera *La Fille du Régiment* is unquestionably a highlight in the young singer's discography. With it Pavarotti delighted a connoisseur like John Steane and managed to move him to what might be considered an overdrawn comparison. There's no doubt the then thirty-two-year-old hit his C's with verve and ease, but they couldn't compare with the brilliance and energy with which Leon Escalaïs once sang them. Still, Pavarotti's singing on this recording is marked by a relaxation and a charm rarely to be heard in later years, even though he's obviously not at home in the French language. It does indicate, however, that an artist with a good instinct for phrasing can lend expression to his singing even in a foreign language he has learned purely phonetically.

That same year Pavarotti recorded Verdi's Requiem under Georg Solti in Vienna. The disc confirms his words that he had practiced the "Hostias" and the "Ingemisco" hundreds of times for Karajan as well as for the memorial performance for Arturo Toscanini. Pavarotti is the only soloist who stands out in a less than homogeneous quartet: Joan Sutherland proves to be a delicately singing but glaringly ill-chosen cast member, Marilyn Horne has a disinterested air, Martti Talvela comes across as uninspired. Pavarotti has several big vocal moments, such as the delicate shading of "qui Mariam" in "Ingemisco" and the floating notes in the "Hostias," but I have to agree with Alan Blyth, who feels that this is singing with one's heart on one's sleeve, that is, more for effect than inwardly restrained.[1]

To summarize, then: In the early years Pavarotti's voice was that of a lean, bright lyric tenor without the dark red-wine modulations of the baritones who had been favored only a short time before. It was a voice with an easy extension to the higher range, a limited color palette, and a relatively undeveloped *agilità*. In a conversation with Helena Matheopoulos, Pavarotti himself described bel canto as the best control, even as medicine for the voice, but when he describes "a smooth, even flow of liquid, well-focused sound" as the ideal, he probably had the technique more in mind than his own voice. One of the curious things about this vocalist's book is that she lets many singers describe and idealize technical rules even though these very singers by no stretch of the imagaination even try to meet them.[2]

It was a full five years after his debut before Pavarotti recorded his first album. This is remarkable. By the end of the 1950s there wasn't much more of a show one could make with Mario del Monaco or even with Giuseppe di Stefano. Jussi Björling had died in 1960. The glorious Verdi stylist Carlo Bergonzi, Franco Corelli, and Richard Tucker were the dominant singers on the Italian scene. In 1966 Pavarotti sang the role of Orombello in Bellini's *Beatrice di Tenda* alongside Joan Sutherland. The following six years saw the addition of Tonio in *La Fille du Régiment* (1967), Verdi's Requiem under Solti, Fritz Kobus in Mascagni's *L'Amico Fritz* (1968) under Gianandrea Gavazzeni, Richard Strauss's *Der Rosenkavalier* (1969) under Solti, Verdi's *Un Ballo in Maschera* (1970) under Bruno Bartoletti, Donizetti's *L'Elisir d'Amore* (1970) and *Lucia di Lammermoor* (1971) under Richard Bonynge, Verdi's *Macbeth* (1971) under Lamberto Gardelli, Giacomo Puccini's *La Bohème* (1972) under Herbert von Karajan, *Turandot* (1972) under Zubin Mehta, and finally the Duke in Verdi's *Rigoletto* (1972) under Richard Bonynge—for a grand total of twelve albums in the space of six years. This marked Pavarotti's rise to the ranks of stardom.

With a few exceptions, Pavarotti remained within his discipline until the end of the 1960s. In 1973 he sang Arturo in *I Puritani*, in 1974 Fernando in Donizetti's *La Favorita*, in 1974–75 Leicester in Donizetti's *Maria Stuarda* under Richard Bonynge. In addition to these roles from the romantic repertoire he also sang Pinkerton in Puccini's *Madama Butterfly* (1974) under Herbert von Karajan, Rodolfo in Verdi's *Luisa Miller* (1975) under Peter Maag, and Manrico in Verdi's *Il Trovatore* (1976) under Richard Bonynge, as well as the verismo pair: Pietro Mascagni's *Cavalleria Rusticana* under Gianandrea Gavazzeni and Ruggiero Leoncavallo's *Pagliacci* under Giuseppe Patané.

In 1978, finally, the tenor tried his hand at a hybrid role, that of Arnoldo in Rossini's *Guglielmo Tell*. From then on, in addition to his traditional lyric parts such as Alfredo in *La Traviata* (1979) or Elvino in *La Sonnambula* (1980), both under Bonynge, he also undertook a series of more difficult roles: Cavaradossi in *Tosca* (1978), Faust in Arrigo Boito's *Mefistofele* (1980) under the direction of Oliviero de Fabritiis, Enzo in Amilcare Ponchielli's *La Gioconda* (1980) under Bruno Bartoletti, Umberto Giordano's *Andrea Chenier* (1984) under Riccardo Chailly, and the role of Radames in Verdi's

Aïda (1985) under Lorin Maazel as well as that of Pollione in *Norma* (1988) under Bonynge. These were accompanied by second recordings of Verdi's *Un Ballo in Maschera* (1985) under Sir Georg Solti and *Rigoletto* (1989) under Riccardo Chailly, the Verdi Requiem (1988) under Riccardo Muti for EMI and Donizetti's *L'Elisir d'Amore* (1990) for Deutsche Grammophon. What's striking about all of this is that there are no complete recordings during the years between 1981 and 1984, with the exception of Mozart's *Idomeneo*. This is apparently one consequence of the vocal crisis already alluded to.

Two masses by Rossini have to be added to this growing list, as well as recitals of old Italian arias and romantic lieder along with appropriate Neapolitan songs and, within the past few years, live recordings of concerts. These latter discs hardly justify their publication when measured against their artistic or documentary quality, but they certainly meet the current market standards. In the sections that follow, these recordings will not be discussed chronologically, but rather grouped according to their stylistic method, all the while keeping in mind the question of whether or not Pavarotti's voice did justice to the respective roles.

MOZART AND MATTERS
OF STYLE

John Pritchard's 1983 digital studio production was first
published in 1988. . . . It has a very curious, old-fashioned
effect. Pritchard conducts . . . a syrupy, phlegmatic, sono-
rously harmonious and autumnal Idomeneo, which . . . is
as exciting as a visit to the ancient civilization exhibit in
the British Museum. . . . Luciano Pavarotti is the only
one to resist—even if with the ineffectual means of a
zealous italianità—*the reserved tendency of the*
whole undertaking.

ATTILA CSAMPAI, *Idomeneo*

N o other term is as frequently deployed against artists as the word *style*, and this, in turn, most particularly when the topic under discussion is the work of
Wolfgang Amadeus Mozart. It has occasioned such global
prejudices as "Italian singers can't sing Mozart," or the spu-
rious remark that Karl Böhm performed the operas of his
favorite composer "stylishly." At the same time, Nikolaus

Harnoncourt's forward-looking "back to history" approach was being praised as a way of introducing a "new Mozart style" while avoiding a precise evaluation among the critics of its consequences for the execution of the vocal parts. Harald Goertz published a two-part essay titled "Unser Unfug mit Mozart" (Our mischief with Mozart) in *Opernwelt*, in which he convincingly demonstrated the need for a fundamental stylistic overhaul. Be that as it may, the stylish as well as the styleless Mozart vocalists continue to haunt these critical reviews. The former hail exclusively from Vienna or Munich, the latter from Italy or New York. What these reviews do not discuss is that English singers, for example, execute the formal language of Mozart's music with more precision than do many of their German colleagues, or that, to give another example, the Mozart performances under Sir Colin Davis, especially as regards the vocal parts, are infinitely more differentiated and more richly nuanced—more stylish, in other words—than those of Karl Böhm.

In his book *The Art of Singing*, the ever-pragmatic and ever-sensible William James Henderson tells us, "The manner of singing Mozart is not the manner of singing Puccini, nor will the manner suitable for Donizetti be found appropriate to the lyric dramas of Wagner." Henderson contrasts his concept of "manner" with that of "matter," by which he means the unchanging technique and method of singing. To quote him again: "There is only one right way to sing, in so far as the technics of the voice are meant." The moment in which

Donna Anna recognizes Giovanni for her father's murderer demands dramatic declamation, just as David's lecture before Stolzing requires a polished bel canto style—yet this is but one technique that makes possible the transformation of spoken language into completely and fully realized music. Henderson discusses style from two different angles (which also happen to be the titles of separate sections of his book): "Style and Recitative" and "The Lyric in Style." "Singers of the eighteenth century . . . were invariably praised for the purity and equality of their tone, their breath power, their *messa di voce*, their *portamento*, their smooth and beautiful execution of runs and other florid passages and for their trills."[1]

These abilities alone allow for a stylish performance of Mozart's vocal parts or of those enchanting old Italian arias that Pavarotti is so fond of singing in his concerts. They are also indispensible for any performance of Bellini's aria-like songs, as well as those of Donizetti, Tosti, or Respighi, not to mention the Neapolitan songs.[2]

Pavarotti has sung only two Mozart roles during his entire career: the first was Idamante in Glyndebourne and later the title role in *Idomeneo*, for a total of seven performances starting in October 1982 in New York, another six in July and August of the next year in Salzburg. The sound recording was cut in Vienna in June and September 1983, and even if John Pritchard and not James Levine was the person in charge in the studio, one can probably assume that Pavarotti's interpretation was not subjected to any alterations.

The reviews varied: "The uncontested star among the golden throats assembled here is naturally 'Big P.,' who cuts a good figure as a Mozart tenor, even if theatrical pressure drives the otherwise very intense portrayal of the King of Crete wrestling with fate to the very limits of Mozartian good taste. He feels more at home in the arias than in the ensembles, where his voice is sometimes too dominant."[3] "The perfectly cast title role all too frequently [forced] the tenor, who has a rather narrow range in the high notes, to strain."[4] "Luciano Pavarotti singing Mozart—a special case, certainly an experiment, but a successful one, as his *Idomeneo* at the New York Met and the Salzburg Festival proved. . . . The part is surely a borderline role for the singer, lying in a stylistic realm beyond his own unique domain. But in Mozart's Italian operas *italianità* is no alien element, for the composer surely had a great deal of experience with Italian singers who introduced this quality into their performance. Even the sound recording shows: when a singing personality like Pavarotti takes on the role of Idomeneo, the portrayal gains credibility and presence through his vocal and theatrical stature."[5]

Such pseudocritics can be quoted ad nauseam. Why, for example, can't we ever find even one single reference as to how the singer handles "Fuor del mar," that masterful aria which Hermann Jadlowker once sang with coloratura perfectly integrated into the line and the spirit of the piece? Pavarotti handles several coloratura flights very well and without any aspirations, but they have the effect of being tacked on, like veils. There is only the hint of a trill on "minacciar," but it doesn't oscillate evenly. The intonation on "è sì vicino" is not quite clean, and again and again the phrases ending in a consonant resound with an abrupt exhalation of breath. This makes the performance sound strained and forced, which has less to do with *italianità* than with the voice that, because tired and dull, is not agile enough to react and whose rhythmic variation leaves just about everything to be desired.

No, Pavarotti's difficulties with Mozart can't be pinned on a vague concept of style or some arbitrary reference to an alleged *italianità*. He who sings out less energetically than, say, Werner Hollweg (with a smaller voice) can hardly be accused of tasteless aberrations. He does have some technical problems in producing the holy trinity of tone, dynamic variation, and agility, though. Pavarotti's technique derives not from the formal world of bel canto but from the nature of the music since Donizetti and Verdi. This can be seen clearly in recitals that require what William James Henderson has called "the lyric in style." Since an album called *Pavarotti in Concert* came out in 1974 but was presumably recorded the year before, one can make one's own judgment regarding the technical skills of the still relatively young singer. He guards against the slips in taste that lent Benjamino Gigli's renditions of the older vocal music so cloyingly sweet: the rustling falsettos, the sobbed "emotional gushes," the aspirations, the whole masquerade of dripping sentimentality. No, artistry and taste are both in evidence in his vocal execution—but it doesn't fit in all that well with the caustic, unrefined arrangements of songs by Bellini, Tosti, and Respighi by some close relative of Mr. Mantovani or Henry Mancini.

The recital begins with "Per la gloria d'adorarvi" from *Griselda*, melody by Bononcini and orchestral bubble bath by Douglas Gamley. Beautiful, calm rendition of the first phrase and its expressive repetition in *piano*. A good trill on "care." However, as soon as the voice has to climb to the F in "penerò, v'amerò"—in other words, in the *passaggio* zone—it loses all substance in its attempt to produce a *piano*. It sounds breathy and dull; the tone has no shape, no musical contour. This is even more evident in Handel's "Care selve" from *Atalanta*, once sung by John McCormack with the golden tones of Kreisler's violin. The phrase ending with "cor" just before the reprise is accompanied by an ugly gasp, and the leap to the A is just as strained as is the attempt to fade off with a diminuendo. What is missing here is once again "the lyric in style." Equally insufferable is how Pavarotti takes the easy way out with aspirations, especially in his attempts to sing *piano* in the *passaggio* register. Even the arrangements of the songs of Bellini, Tosti, and Respighi—truly tender, intimate, reserved vocal pieces—are meant to conform to the cultural scene of the Hollywood Bowl or of a film like *Yes, Giorgio*, with which Pavarotti made a fool of himself even in the eyes of his most ardent fans. Finally, in Rossini's "La Danza," where he is supposed to unleash the glories of the tenor voice, all he manages to do is master the quick leaps to the high A's. The rest is just vocal struggles with a piece whose whole effect depends on its being "laid down" with a profusion of sound and great rhythmic energy.

Do the Neapolitan songs belong here, in the context of Mozart and style? Those songs that oscillate so curiously between art song and street ballad? It's easy, all too easy, to denigrate the popular in the name of good taste and "high" art, and it requires eminent skills, a sublime appreciation of art and "something in the heart" (Caruso) to transform "Core 'ngrato" into an expression of heart-rending sorrow. These songs of sun and sea, of broken hearts and unrequited love, can't be wrapped in the deceptive cloaks of faddish arrangements, can't be transplanted into a nightclub atmosphere with hosts and hostesses at the mike. The charm of the old recordings of Fernando de Lucia and Enrico Caruso, Riccardo Stracciari and Tito Schipa, lies precisely in the fact that one can hear and feel the echo of Naples—that one can wander around its streets in one's mind and soul, something that holiday makers are no longer able to do on tour. If someone today wants to conjure up the atmosphere of days gone by, he or she has to let these songs beseech in their own soft way, has to let them overwhelm with the heavy sweetness of memory. Pavarotti exposes them, as it were, to the magnifying glass of the microphone. In league with the arranger, he kneads them for the hotel lounge or the pizza parlor where, ever since his voice has become interwoven into the tapestry of mundane Muzak, they function as Italian pillars of sound. What doesn't escape the sharp scrutiny of the mike, however, is that here, too, he has problems with the technical nuances described above.

PAVAROTTI AND ROSSINI

*The elder David, father of the present artist, whose voice
once enjoyed a reputation equal to that of his son, is constantly reproaching the latter for not singing with sufficient
sweetness, and for sacrificing too much vocal quality in
the cause of mere technical acrobatics.*

STENDHAL

*I*t was Gioachino Rossini, we recall, who inserted parts in
the highest tessitura into his Neapolitan operas, and
primarily for Giovanni David, who was born sometime between 1788 and 1790 to Giacomo David, an even more baritone-like tenor who had a singing technique that was, by all
descriptions, phenomenal. In his essay "Heroes on the Rise,"
Stefan Zucker quotes one of the elder David's contemporaries: "He is most appreciated in arias of strength, bravura and
surprise. The most treacherous leaps, the most difficult into-
nations, the most intricate cadenzas, semitone trills—feats
not to be expected from anyone else in his sphere . . . all are
for Davidde [*sic*] ease, manner and grace."[1]

The elder David was the founder of a school of singers commanding a range of two and a half octaves; they were, of course, his son Giovanni David and Andrea Nozzari. The latter in turn became the teacher of Giovanni Battista Rubini. Nozzari sang in nine operas Rossini wrote for the Teatro San Carlo in Naples between 1815 and 1822: *Elisabetta, Regina d'Inghilterra; Otello; Armida; Mosè in Egitto; Riccardo e Zoraide; Ermione; La Donna del Lago; Maometto II;* and *Zelmira*. Although according to his students, Nozzari was fundamentally a baritone whose voice went down as far as the low G, he could also reach a high D. In several operas, including *Otello*, he sang next to the younger David, "the only true tenor of our generation" (Stendhal), who mastered a range of three octaves in his performances. Bellini wrote an F‴ for him in his *Bianca è Fernando*, but he managed to reach as high as the A and the B flat. That can have been technically possible only if he used the *voce mista* or a falsetto, which, *da capo* for Richard Bonynge, was more sharply focused than the one Pavarotti produced in *I Puritani*.

Pavarotti sang none of those roles in which such tenors as Ernesto Palacio, Chris Merritt, Raùl Gimènez, Giuseppe Morino, or Salvatore Fisichella dazzled recent audiences with their occasionally brilliant coloratura. Nor did he sing the darker part of Otello (mastered with extraordinary confidence by the young José Carreras). He thus never attempted one of the integral components of bel canto music at all, although training in singing such runs would have been very helpful for his voice, which was often kept tense and taut.

Such coloratura can be heard only in Rossini's Stabat Mater, the *Petite Messe Solennelle*, and *Guglielmo Tell*. In the Stabat Mater Pavarotti takes the high phrases all the way up to the D flat without any obvious effort, but the tone sounds tense; it doesn't flow as freely as it did from the young Björling, who also lent the phrases more depth—the "third dimension"—with a much more suspenseful portamento. Pavarotti certainly didn't approach his only Rossini role, that of Arnoldo in *Guglielmo Tell*, with the vocal elegance that continued to distinguish Nicolai Gedda's singing even after the Swede's voice was beginning to show signs of wear and tear. Gedda's phrases have more nuance and expression and are infinitely more flexible in their dynamics. Gedda frequently, but not always, uses the *voce mista* in the upper register, reminding us once again of Nourrit's style.

On the other hand, as Richard Osborne writes in *Opera on Record*, Pavarotti succumbs to his "habit of making everything above the staff shine" and thus robs the music of its more delicate coloration.[2] The reaction among critics varied, but on the whole it wasn't positive. Ulrich Schreiber reproached the singer as well as the conductor with "sloppy phrasing" and of having fallen into the "shallows of taste." The reason may be the stylistic transplant: the "elegant French version" was reduced to an Italian "red-blooded

reading" (Osborne) not far removed from a coarse melodrama. An objective comparison of "Asil héréditaire" (Italian: "O muto asil"), which is equally challenging for any
voice, must favor Gedda as the by far more richly nuanced
singer.[3] He takes pains not only to make a dolce leap up
to "hérédi-*taire*," as did Tamagno in his day, but also to
incorporate the subtle shadings that one vainly seeks in
Pavarotti; this is also because Pavarotti's voice, which long
ago ceased to float on the breath, reaches such heights only
under the greatest pressure. The result is those jarring musical contrasts between his confident, steeled, and translucent *acuti* and the tones formed with a semivoice, which
emerge dull, almost like a whisper, in the middle register.

As far as the first and fundamental quality of singing is
concerned, Pavarotti's tonal formation is not free. Whenever he tries to lighten a soft tone or sound, the lower
resonance, the basis of the sound, seemingly disappears.
Thus there can never develop a homogenous legato, by
definition the perfectly smooth transition from one tone to
another on every rhythmic level. Equally striking is that
the strong compression of the *forte* tones again and again
leads to an exhalation at the end of each phrase. The recording of the trio gives the impression that high-pressure
singing is what it's all about—even though Signori
Pavarotti, Sherrill Milnes, and Nicolai Ghiaurov never even
approximated the brilliantly sustained performance Giovanni Martinelli, Giuseppe de Luca, and José Mardones

gave when they sang it.⁴ I share Osborne's view that the conductor, Richard Chailly, presents the work from Verdi's perspective, but I have difficulty in deriving pleasure from the raucousness and the potentially violent tempi.

PAVAROTTI AND BELLINI

*A musical drama must make people weep, shudder, die
through the singing . . . singing has to move people to tears.*

VINCENZO BELLINI in a letter
to Count Carlo Pepoli

𝒫 avarotti's stage repertoire includes two roles from
Vincenzo Bellini: Elvino in *La Sonnambula* and Arturo in *I Puritani*. He sang the former with Joan Sutherland
as his partner on the London stage in 1965, and the latter for
the first time in Catania in 1968, then in Philadelphia in 1972,
and after that another ten performances at the Met in 1976.
He recorded *I Puritani*, Bellini's last opera, in 1973 and sang
the lighter role of Elvino for the first time on tape in 1980
when Joan Sutherland recorded her second rendition of
Amina (Nicola Monti was her partner on the first recording).
The third and fourth Bellini roles to be recorded were those
of Orombello in *Beatrice di Tenda* (1966), more of a talent test
than anything else, and Pollione in *Norma*.

Elvino as well as Arturo are both Rubini roles, the first a

gracefully lyric one with delicate *fioriture* and various ornaments, primarily suspensions and *gruppetti*. A 1976 duet recording with Joan Sutherland gives an idea of how his Elvino
could have sounded: Pavarotti begins the recitative and the
first phrases of "Prendi, l'anel ti dono" carefully and melodiously, but with a tone that is too veiled to allow the cantilena
to emerge in full bloom. For Sutherland, who was no longer
singing this role onstage, the complete recording came too
late, but for the tenor it came much too late. She no longer
had at her disposal the sweetly elegaic, hoveringly delicate
tone of her vocal prime. He, on the other hand, suffered from
a dimished dynamic range and difficulties producing a sub-
stantial legato line, not to mention a lack of that vocal elegance, that fluid stream and virtuosity one associated with
Cesare Valletti, who not only proved to be a master tenor—
what a wonderfully ornate rendition of "Son geloso del
zeffiro," combined with the proper direction of the voices in
the sextet—but also produced the delicate sound of a *tenore
di grazia* at all dynamic levels. All of this can still be heard
on the 1955 recording Valletti made with Maria Callas under
the direction of Leonard Bernstein. Pavarotti's B flats and
C's, sung with the full voice, sound not only constricted and
strained but almost strangled, and that, to put it mildly, is
counterproductive in a melodic line that personifies lyricism
at its height. The listener is deprived of all possibility of
abandoning himself to the sweet sorrow of being moved to
tears by a lyric melody.

According to the majority of critics, Pavarotti was in top form when he sang the role of Arturo for the 1973 recording. Nevertheless, this critic's eyes didn't fill with tears they way those of Heinrich Heine and Prince Metternich did at the sound of the high falsetto F, which literally wrung eulogies of praise for the tenor from Luca Fontana. Just how differently the individual critics reacted to this extreme note and the way it was produced can be seen in the verdict of Ulrich Schreiber, who heard only "a horrible falsetto."[1] Far from looking for the truth where one seldom finds it, namely in the middle, I am of the opinion that, when it comes to this note, one would do best to settle for some sort of expedient. It's generally very difficult to integrate such a high note into today's vocal performances. Perhaps singers ought to follow the example of Alfred Kraus, who, under Riccardo Muti, let it go with a well-concentrated high D flat. Even Nicolai Gedda, to whom Richard Fairman in *Opera on Record* concedes elements of "Rubini's elegance,"[2] produced a high F that I find remarkable but certainly not "transporting," as Schreiber describes it—and this despite the admirable technique of producing the tone by means of a concentrated and well-supported *voix mixte*.

Back then, when I first heard and above all when I compared Pavarotti's performance against the Arturo that Giuseppe di Stefano sang without any finesse at all, I was impressed not only by his execution but also by his linear phrasing and controlled energy, especially since his voice on this recording lacks the harsh and constricted sound it has on many others. Even so, as John Steane says, standards are established through comparison, and a comparison with the recordings of the stylistically untouchable Alessandro Bonci, whose C sharp in the second stanza of "A te, o cara" is pure magic, as well as a comparison with the recordings of Giacomo Lauri-Volpi, who is distinguished by his elegant bravado, leaves Pavarotti at the starting gate, for he hardly ever tries to soften or animate his phrases with a *messa di voce*. His is no swaggeringly sensitive Arturo; rather, he presents himself as a self-confident, singing happy-go-lucky. Even so, this recording, with Sutherland in very good form, is one of the best he has ever made. On the other hand, Piero Cappuccili and Nicolai Ghiaurov fall far behind the standards once established by Mattia Battistini (in "In sogno beato," for example) or even Ezio Pinza (in "Cinta di fiori"), whereby the baritone is the energetically singing virtuoso and the bass the master of a subtly shaded cantabile.

Some great singers continued to record well past their prime—Adelina Patti, Marcella Sembrich, or Lilli Lehmann come to mind—and these records give us an idea of the glory that was. They are important for preserving the old style or the great tradition, and in this sense they are indispensable. I wonder if anyone will ever look upon Joan Sutherland's second recording of *Norma* from this perspective. The Australian first sang the aria in a recital in 1960, then again in 1964 in a complete recording under the direction of Richard

Bonynge. The first rendition was brilliant and featured a translucent, silvery, accomplished tone, which later, as Andrew Porter writes in his discography, gives way to a phrasing "con intenzione" and to a darker, cloudier sound.[3] Like Porter I also find Sutherland's mezza voce by far less expressive and "beautiful" than the soft sound of Callas, which did indeed fill my eyes with the tears Bellini demanded. There is but little of the earlier brilliance to be heard on this new recording, and nothing, absolutely nothing, of dramatic declamation, an ability that never was her strong point in any case.

And Pavarotti? He who could have been an ideal Pollione doesn't come through with his typically energetic combination of singing and acting skills and doesn't even hold his own when compared to the stylistically less accomplished Franco Corelli (with Maria Callas, 1960) or John Alexander (with Joan Sutherland, 1964). One senses that the recording studio wanted to return a favor or honor a contractual agreement with the diva and to mitigate the disaster to a certain extent by featuring well-known names guaranteed to attract an audience. The result is an unmitigated catastrophe.

PAVAROTTI AND DONIZETTI

I love Verdi's music, but my voice loves Donizetti's roles.

LUCIANO PAVAROTTI

*T*he work of Gaetano Donizetti is particularly interesting for the development of vocal music. This prolific
composer was both hero and victim of his contemporary
theater scene; he wrote approximately seventy operas, created
the type of the dark mezzo-soprano in his French works (for
the great Teresa Stolz), and filled the region between tenor
and bass with a middle voice called the baritone, which was
practically unknown to Mozart and Bellini. The first typical
baritone part is probably Rossini's barber of Seville, but Donizetti was the first to define the conditions and the gender
specifications of his stage figures as far as timbre and pitch
were concerned. After the castrato, the role of the lover was
finally lost to the "alto in pants." The tenor became the
symbol for youth, eros, and passion, while the roles of the
husband, the jealous suitor, and the sinister antagonist and
villain were assigned to the baritone. The *basso cantante*, who

up until then had sung Mozart's Don Giovanni and Figaro, and even more so the *basso profondo* were cast in the roles of father figures, kings, potentates, and priests, or else, for those with the darkest color, in the role of infernal figures (Caspar in *Freischütz*, Sparafucile in *Rigoletto*).

In keeping with the psychologically realistic character of the romantic melodrama, the women's roles were also defined along psychological lines and physiological capabilities. The translucent first soprano was cast as innocent and pure youth; her antagonist—exaggerated to figures such as Azucena, Eboli, and Amneris in Verdi's works and Ortrud in the role of the evil (because political) woman in Wagner—was sung by the mezzo-soprano; while the altos, whom Rossini used in his ornate and florid songs, were always assigned the role of page because of their *jeux d'esprit*.

As far as the tenor roles were concerned, Donizetti increasingly eliminated the ornamental elements (which could always be found in Bellini's works) whenever he wrote for Giovanni David (*Bianca è Fernando*) or for Rubini.

In his *History of Bel Canto*, Rodolfo Celletti tells us:

> Donizetti, on the other hand, uses coloratura[1] whenever he is writing for Rubini, and this applies not only to youthful operas, but also to *Anna Bolena* (Percy) and *Marin Faliero* (Fernando). He also uses it, quite often, in parts written for the tenor Duprez, but only until Duprez set himself up as the imitator of Rubini. . . . Later on, the roles written for Duprez diverged in the direction of a studiously plain type of com-

position—Edgardo in *Lucia*, Fernando in *La Favorita*, Poliuto in *Martyrs*, and Don Sebastiano. For another of his great interpreters, the tenor Napoleone Moriani, Donizetti confined himself to plain singing. . . . It should be noted also that the coloratura of the roles composed by Bellini and Donizetti for Rubini or "first-manner" Duprez is infinitely less bold and acrobatic than that of Rossini. To offset this, the tessitura is exceptionally high, both in vocalise singing and in syllabic singing. But it was Donizetti—with Duprez in his second manner (from *Lucia* onwards) and with Moriani—who was to fix the real tessitura of the Romantic tenor, high, certainly, but not excessively high, passing it on later to Verdi.[2]

The Donizetti roles as well as those of the young Verdi obviously provided Pavarotti with the best opportunity to develop his talents. The first to be mentioned in this regard is the superb recording of *La Fille du Régiment*, which was followed three years later by *L'Elisir d'Amore* with Joan Sutherland as a rather weepy Adina (her elegaic, teary singing is out of tune with the capricious character) and two other, less distinct voices for Belcore and Dulcamara. What wouldn't we give to hear singers like Tito Gobbi, Renato Capecchi or such a glorious *buffa* interpreter as Giuseppe Taddei instead of Dominic Cossa and Spiro Malas, especially since the duets have to be acted out vocally. Harold Rosenthal wrote a positive review of the complete recording which was made under the supervision of Richard Bonynge (and which includes a vocal waltz reminiscent of performances featuring

Maria Malibran). Rosenthal said that not only did Pavarotti sing "Quanto è bella" unreservedly and intimately enough, but his "Una furtiva lagrima" would "melt a stone."[3]

As far as "Quanto è bella" is concerned, I am reminded of a statement Maria Callas made after one of her first performances as Norma: "The performance was not as good as I sang it in my imagination."[4] The recordings give no indication of how sweet and soft, how pensive and energetic this brief piece can sound. Gigli, no longer a young singer, caresses the phrases with his honey-sweet mezza voce but interpolates an overdynamic and even slightly tremulous high note. Perhaps the young Ferruccio Tagliavini came closest to the ideal, with a tone equally soft and sensuous.

Pavarotti's coloring of the sound comes across as unimaginative in contrast, and this, too, is dependent on the techniques of both tone production and dynamic shading. In the romance I miss not only the subtly colored nuances and the *messa di voce* effects but also the spontaneous, free play with the trills that so characterizes the Caruso recording of 1904 as *hors concours*.[5] There's no doubt Pavarotti sings the romance with more effect than Nicola Monti, with more clarity than Giuseppe di Stefano, infinitely more melodiously than Luigi Alva, more stylishly than Rudolf Schock, with a warmer tone than Nicolai Gedda, who here sounds dull and indifferent; but he reserves his best for the duets and the ensembles: buoyancy, rhythmic accentuation, and flexible diction.

The recording under the direction of James Levine, who held back on brilliance and brio, can be described as yet another reissue, as it were, of an infinitely repeated production. Not that Pavarotti comes across as routine, for he seems to be much too enamored of the part for that. But time has acquainted him with Nemorino on his good as well as his bad days. After three decades on the stage, where should he reap, today, more sensuous sweetness for "Quanto è bella," where should he find more technical freedom, brilliance, and energy for "Una furtiva"? No, his Nemorino is still a great guy, but a little dotty next to Kathleen Battle's agile Adina. One wonders whether, after the wedding, he'll be sitting in the tavern with Enzo Dara's Dulcamara and feeling like Don Pasquale? To be fair, we have to say that Pavarotti's Nemorino is perceived onstage rather the way he portrayed him under the direction of Jean-Pierre Ponnelle, which is to say, as a simultaneously naive yet witty lad, as a loveable teddy bear and self-confident charmer possessed of a versatility that comes from the inner dynamics of singing. I remember his performance in Hamburg as a superb demonstration of vocal and dramatic theater.

The second principal Donizetti role, Edgardo in *Lucia di Lammermoor*, goes back to Duprez. Pavarotti recorded it in 1971 and truly was in top form at the time. With the exception of the last scene of the opera, "Tu che a Dio spiegasti l'ali," once sung with more subtle portamenti and more delicate lyric nuances by John McCormack, this role lets the singer come out of his shell in a direct and convincing way.

Pavarotti doesn't go as far as did Giuseppe di Stefano, whom he clearly eclipses, especially in the nuances he lends to the recitative. Here, it seems to me, he strikes an almost ideal balance between lyric yet energetic singing, controlled yet animated phrasing, and unstrained brilliance. The brilliant Joan Sutherland could hardly have wished for a better partner on this recording.

Pavarotti sang the role of Fernando in *La Favorita* nowhere nearly as often as that of Edgardo; but it was only to be expected that the part, first learned for San Francisco (1973–74) and later repeated in Bologna, was slated for recording. Today's musical world functions according to the maxim of concentrating the means and extending the effect, with the result that hardly any of the singer's stage roles is not already, at least potentially, immortalized on disc.

A deliberate component of the promotional strategy was to release the recording at exactly the time the work was being repeated at the Met. But was it really revived, the way Maria Callas revitalized some of Donizetti's other works— *Lucia*, for instance, or *Anna Bolena*? Despite its title, the opera is written not for the mezzo-soprano but for the tenor. The last Met performance worthy of note took place on December 29, 1905, and featured Enrico Caruso as Fernando, Edyth Walker as Leonora, and such luminaries as Antonio Scotti and Pol Plançon in the ensemble. As early as the aria in the first act, "Una vergine, un angel di Dio," Pavarotti was able to rise to the height of a D flat, and he also interpolated this note in the martial cabaletta toward the end of that same act. It was effective, but here too the production of these *acuti* was a little strained, and that made them sound a bit constricted. Lacking above all in the glorious romance "Spirto gentil," once buoyantly and wonderfully balanced by Caruso between bel canto song and dramatic *espressivo*, was what the trade calls "poise," the uninhibited flow of the breath that carries the note and with it the potential for coloring and portamenti. Disturbing, too, are the gasps at the end of the sustained and highly compressed top notes.

I wonder, though, if when making comparisons like this, the critic is justified in always referring to one or two standard recordings. There are two such recordings that date from the 1950s: Alberto Erede recorded the work for Decca with Gianni Pogi, who was responsible for having produced for disc several of the ugliest, most gutteral, clunkiest sounds in the history of tenors. The other album features Gianni Raimondi on a Cetra recording under the direction of Angelo Questa. He was another singer with brilliant pitch, but as far as fluidity and slurring in singing and elegance of manner are concerned, Pavarotti clearly surpasses him. Unfortunately, in Fiorenza Cosotto Pavarotti had a partner with insecure intonation in the high position, and even Nicolai Ghiaurov, still basking in self-satisfied appreciation of his own voice, didn't elevate the standard either, which was historically controversial to start with and could have aroused renewed interest in opera.

Donizetti's three operas about the Tudor queens have been gaining in popularity ever since the 1957 revival of *Anna Bolena* at the Teatro alla Scala with Maria Callas singing the title role. There may be a very practical reason for this, for the successors of the Greek—Elena Suliotis, Montserrat Caballé, Beverly Sills, and Renata Scotto—needed fresh and unprecedented roles in their repertoire. In addition to *Anna Bolena*, the Schiller opera *Maria Stuarda* and *Roberto Devereux* have no performance history behind them that could serve as model, mainly because they disappeared from the stage in the 1880s. Each of these works has turned up in the meantime in four or even five different versions, all of which have been tailored to meet modern stage requirements; thus they represent a compromise from a historical point of view. This is especially true for the recording of *Maria Stuarda* under the direction of Richard Bonynge, an opera that was composed in 1834 for San Carlo in Naples, then fell victim to the censor and was finally reworked for a performance in Milan with Maria Malibran. Both earlier versions have been lost, so that one has to rely upon a printed edition dating back to 1855 Paris (see Jeremy Commons's notes accompanying the recording for details).

Like *Anna Bolena*, *Maria Stuarda* stands and falls with the acting ability of the title figure and her antagonist, Queen Elizabeth. As in Schiller's drama of the same name, which was concerned with idealizing reality, the meeting between the two rivals is the climax of the piece—and both Joan

Sutherland and Huguette Tourangeau know how to make the most of it. This meeting, by the way, is a dramatic invention and completely devoid of historic verification. Bonynge dressed up the parts of both protagonists with a rich and elegant accompaniment, and the quality of Joan Sutherland's acting justified the performance. She sings with a rich tone, sparkling energy in the caballettas and delicate decorations in the cantabile lines, but because of her notorious indifference to the formal power of consonants, her performance lacks the eloquence that made the Callas recording so memorable. This particular role was technically arranged to match the artistic capabilities of the Canadian mezzo-soprano, so that she at times sounds like the most glorious female bass-baritone since Zarah Leander.

On the whole, Pavarotti's work is flawless. Of course, he still sings as he always has done ever since the mid-1970s, which is to say, with a relatively solid, metallic, and not always fluid tone. Noteworthy, too, is the narrowly focused pitch, which has a slightly rigid effect or, paradoxically, can sound tortured and brilliant at the same time, especially since it was obviously of great importance to the singer at that time to serve up a C or, at the end of the duet with the heroine in the second act, a D flat. This tendency toward self-direction, however, is compensated by a good linear formation and, as always, by his outstanding and impeccable diction.

PAVAROTTI AND VERDI

Everyone knows the nickname given to Verdi: the Attila of the voice. Less well known is the fact that before Verdi, Bellini was accused of having ruined by his method of writing three great singers: Henriette Méric-Lalande with Il Pirata *and* La Straniera, *Antonio Tamburini, again with* La Straniera, *and Pasta with* La Sonnambula *and* Norma. . . . *Romantic opera, with its emphasis, its nervous excitement—which reached its peak with Verdi—popularized extremely high notes in chest voice (perhaps even "screams from the soul," as someone has called them, but also the purveyors of drama and gladiatorial encounter on the stage); it encouraged stentorian vocalism, indeed, it almost made a virtue of it, reinforcing the orchestral texture, introducing unison of voices with voices and voices with instruments; it suppressed agility singing for tenors, baritones, and basses and encouraged singers to abandon it even for study purposes, with disastrous consequences as far as spontaneity of emission and flexibility and softness of tone were concerned. . . . Furthermore, encouraging the cult of a certain immediate, all-consuming expressiveness, it favoured certain interpretative values in preference to vocal and virtuoso values, discouraging even women's voices from the sound study of agility singing and spreading amongst singers a certain vulgarity of expression and*

phrasing, over and above the circus-like athleticism of
stentorian high notes held till the breath ran out.

RODOLFO CELLETTI, *A History of Bel Canto*

*M*usical poetry of the purest perfection: an enchanting *andantino*, 6/8 time, originally orches-
trated only for pizzicato strings, with the clarinet and the
bassoon adding their voices at the cadenza. The finest orchestral texture carrying the tenor voice: "Ah, sì, ch'io senta
ancora . . . Dal più remoto esilio" from Giuseppe Verdi's *I
Due Foscari*, which premiered on November 3, 1844, at the
Teatro Argentina in Rome with Giacomo Roppa singing the
role of Jacopo.

The aria will be familiar to aficionados of Verdi's operas
and, like a vocal jewel, equally as precious. The young
Pavarotti sang it in his 1968 recital under the direction of
Edward Downes, but somehow it's never mentioned when
talk turns to "Pavarotti's greatest hits." It ranks as one of his
most beautiful recordings, for he is obviously less concerned
with hitting the high notes than with transforming the
highly ornamented melodic line into vocal calligraphy—not
always impeccable in its slurs, but rich in vocal imagination.
Too bad Pavarotti wasn't part of the recordings that were

being made then of the works of the young Verdi, even though he presumably would have been the right tenor for roles such as that of Oronte in *I Lombardi*, Jacopo in *I Due Foscari*, Carlo in *Giovanna d'Arco*, Foresto in *Attila* and Ernani. At the time of his early operas, the composer was still marching, as it were, to the drums of tradition and, like Bellini and Donizetti, he was composing vocal lines replete with ornate elements. It was only in *Alzira, Il Corsaro*, and *La Battaglia di Legnano* that Verdi introduced the dramatic, declamatory tenor for the first time. He followed this up by steering a middle course in *Luisa Miller, Rigoletto, La Traviata*, and *Un Ballo in Maschera*. These works called for a lyric tenor with an easy extension in pitch and a fairly good volume. These roles stood and continue to stand at the center of Pavarotti's Verdi repertoire. Only later were the roles of Radames and Manrico added, the latter a deep and therefore difficult role despite the C's in the *stretta*. To sing them required an equal measure of lyric as well as dramatic talent. A hybrid role such as that of Arrigo in *I Vespri Siciliani*, a dramatic one like that of Alvaro in *La Forza del Destino*, or even Otello seems to lie beyond Pavarotti's vocal reach. In that sense he is nowhere near as accomplished a Verdi interpreter as Carlo Bergonzi or Giovanni Martinelli and Giacomo Lauri-Volpi once were.

During the first ten years, when his career was still a purely musical one, Pavarotti kept to an iron rule laid down by Nellie Melba: when choosing his parts, he always made sure to sing within his means. This meant that, besides the Duke and Alfredo, which he appropriated during his early years as a singer, he added only one role to his repertoire, namely that of Oronto in *I Lombardi*, and he appeared in it in a total of seven performances at the Rome Opera. In 1971 he added the role of Riccardo from *Ballo* to his repertoire, followed three years later by Rodolfo in *Luisa Miller;* with the role of Manrico in *Il Trovatore* in 1975 he embarked upon the professional switch that so many have come to regret. With a single exception, Pavarotti's Verdi recordings correspond to his vocal development. He recorded *La Traviata* for the first time in 1979, perhaps not too late in his career, but surely at a time when his voice was not in its best condition and responded properly only under pressure. He recorded Riccardo in *Un Ballo in Maschera* at the right time, namely in 1970, and yet not at the right time, because his partners—Renata Tebaldi and Regina Resnik—had little more than their reputation to bring into the studio with them. The recording was completely disqualified because of them, which is all the more regrettable since the tenor gives a model performance. His entrance ("La rivedrà") is elegantly phrased, he sings the technically difficult "Di tu se fedele" with elegance and energy, omits overworked effects like the laugh in "E scherzo od è folia," and manages to find the appropriate tone for the love duet without embellishments. The only fault occurs in the last act, when he doesn't measure up to the incomparable postwar Verdi stylist Carlo Bergonzi, despite his own more impressive voice.

It's difficult to understand how the tenor found grace in the ears of Alan Blyth on his second recording under the direction of Georg Solti. According to Blyth, Pavarotti responds willingly to a part that demands masculine, sensuous singing with extroverted emotionality, and the plaintive quality of his voice is precisely what the role demands. Since Pavarotti sings here with a beaming voice and responds sensitively to most of Verdi's dynamics, one can feel the lightness required by the barcarolle, the zealous attack in the love duet, and the tremendous outpouring of passion in the scene preceding the ball.[1]

True, Pavarotti is obviously taking pains to produce a nuanced, dramatically polished performance, and he works out many details more carefully here than on his first recording. But just about every time, he pushes his voice to the brink of collapse. His attempts to pull back from his *fortissimo* notes lead to dull, breathy, incorporeal sounds, so that many phrases lose their connection through interruptions in the flow. The impression of effort, of strain, is underscored by Solti's hectic tempi and his tendency toward violent crescendos and an expressive overarticulation that robs the work of its inner balance.

Such wide-screen productions of Verdi's music render more than the vocal expression coarse and vulgar. It's thus hard to understand why they are more highly appreciated than such carefully directed, orchestrally conducted performances as that of *Rigoletto* under Richard Bonynge. The latter represents Pavarotti's first-class production of a Verdi opera on record. Not only does he outdistance Jan Peerce, Ferruccio Tagliavini, Mario del Monaco, Jussi Björling, Richard Tucker, Renato Cioni, Carlo Bergonzi, Nicolai Gedda, and all the other tenors who recorded the part after the war, but he also gives a model interpretation of the role, even if it might not fulfill all expectations.

Whoever expects frills in the second stanza of the *ballata* "Questa o quella" and rubato and *messa di voce* shadings in "È il sol dell'anima," whoever waits for soft mezza voce attacks and phrasings in "Parmi veder le lagrime" like the ones Tito Schipa or Ferruccio Tagliavini are famous for, whoever hopes to hear a *gruppetto* à la Caruso on "consolar" at the end of the quartet, is wishing not only for too much but for the impossible. The sum of all these artistic effects would result in a synthetic product. Of course, Pavarotti could sing a little more softly and a bit more carefully here and there; surely several of the semivoiced phrases lack translucence, but all of that is more than balanced by the energetic brilliance of the singing and by a vocal theatricality that brings the character to life on the aural stage. Even Alfredo Kraus, so confident in pitch, hardly sang the D flat at the end of the duet and the D at the end of the cabaletta as brilliantly as the Italian. Joan Sutherland as Gilda is no ominous innocent, unlike the incomparable Maria Callas in the same role, but rather an easygoing country girl, and Sherrill Milnes in the title role causes much embarrassment with his insecure intonation and gravelly sound. On the other hand, the *comprimarii* are outstanding, with Kiri te Kanawa and Martti Talvela as Sparafucile in the vanguard with his raven black voice.

It's astonishing how lively and spontaneously Pavarotti continues to sing the roles that uncontestedly rank among the most difficult of the whole tenor repertoire—even though the D and the D flat sound feigned, and the B sounds strained as well. But what vitality he brings to the very first scene, what power of suggestion oozes through his courting of the Countess Ceprano in their *duettino*! Granted, some tones are constricted, and others break off with an abrupt gasp; granted, some phrasings are more clumsy than elegant. But all of that is outweighed by one of the greatest virtues a singer can have: spontaneity and eloquence. None of this eloquence and presence can be found with, say, a Vincenzo La Scola, who sings the part on a recording under Riccardo Muti that might satisfy opera historians but would fail just about every other test in a live stage production.[2]

When the *Rigoletto* recording under conductor Riccardo Chailly was released, Pavarotti was still the uncontested dominant Italian tenor in his field of *lirico spinto*. What's more, he was also the outstanding singer in the midst of a poorly matched ensemble. Leo Nucci can no longer even suggest, as Julian Budden maintained, that the title role of Rigoletto is the greatest and most glorious role for an Italian lyric-dramatic baritone. The question as to *why* one would make such a recording can be answered only with reference to the constraints of business—or more precisely, of that busy-ness with its contractual obligations that compelled even EMI to produce an additional version with similar casting problems.

Whereas Riccardo Muti fell back upon the new, critical Ricordi edition for his Scala production, released just about simultaneously, and, as usual, swore his singers to a rigid "come scritto," Chailly defended the tradition of vocal freedom, which also, but certainly not only, featured high notes. Muti thus deprives the lead singer of one of the most evocative dramatic effects, which the baritone Felice Varesi had introduced as early as the premiere performance: the fading portamento in "Un vindice avrai." The only performer whom the conductor does allow virtuoso effects doesn't have to sing at all—namely, Riccardo Muti, who not only rushes the *prestissimo* of the aria "Cortigiani" as well as "Si vendetta" but dynamically overheats them as well.

In Chailly's recording, too, there are instances of that kind of "conductor's discretion" that Verdi had already bemoaned in his day: the *stretto* effects in the first scene and later in the duet between Gilda and the Duke, for instance. Now as before, Luciano Pavarotti sings the role superbly: already in the first scene his performance is marked by a certain sting, with supple diction and, in the *duettino* with the Countess Ceprano, with an enchanting, indeed a magnetic wooing in the timbre of his voice. But, unlike the earlier recording, which was the manifestation of a tenor machismo caught by surprise, this version betrays strongly constricted and suddenly explosive tones: the listener's ear perceives the mighty efforts of a slightly exhausted lover.

As far as the aria in the second act is concerned, "Ella mi fu rapita," one need not have a *tenore di grazia* like Tito Schipa in mind to be mildly disappointed. Pavarotti's energetic vocal theatricality lends a high degree of tension to the recitative, but the tones have lost as much in smoothness as have the vowels in sustained timbre. The aria lacks both vocal ease and dynamic nuance. What one hears is a general, hardly ever differentiated, and at times extremely tense and therefore too constricted *forte*. This is even more evident in "Possente amor." Noting that he never consulted the audience as to its preferences, Verdi once said that he had nothing against high notes; his only requisite was that they had to be good. Yet while traversing the taut ropes of the D, the vocal cords vibrate like the wire under an aerialist.

Missing in "La donna è mobile" is that dynamic flexibility that would allow an expressive interpretation of text and melody, and individual accents are repeatedly attacked with too much breathiness. The voice loses its concentration in trying to produce the *piano* nuances in the second verse. In "Bella figlia" one can hear the gradual loosening of a previously controlled vibrato. Finally, I find the manner in which Pavarotti ends a phrase downright disturbing, and it can be heard in many of his late recordings: he breaks off with abrupt gasps of breath that aspirate a vowel in instances that require the production of a voiced consonant.

Would that there were but even a hint of his former spontaneity in the 1979 recording of *La Traviata* under the direction of Richard Bonynge, whose release was postponed for some time (perhaps for corrections?). This is another of those rerecordings that are either granted to or demanded by a diva, and it counts as one of the compromises of a casting policy that believes it can sell an exhausted star better than it can a competent young interpreter. It's also one of those petty annoyances one suffers as an observer of the music industry and a listener to a gramophone that can no longer be switched off. As Alfredo, Pavarotti can't even play the role that he himself has ready to hand, that of a singing charmer, especially when he sings in such bad form as he does here.

Like *Rigoletto*, the recording of *La Traviata* under the direction of James Levine was a second version of the same opera for Pavarotti. The tenor hasn't really managed to expand his repertoire; rather, he continually reproduces his standard roles instead. At the time of the recording, Deutsche Grammophon was evidently trying to pair the extremely busy and thus overtaxed Cheryl Studer with a superstar partner. The soprano, unquestionably a great talent, has said in interviews that she wants to sing as many great roles as possible while she's still young. What she failed to take into consideration is not only the danger of overtaxation but the fact that a voice can age prematurely. She also did not appreciate the fact that roles like those of Violetta or Lucia require stage experience.

Since she had neither performed the role as often as she should have nor worked it out theatrically, the recording came too early for the soprano; for Pavarotti, on the other hand, it came too late. Although on the whole the tenor is in better form on this recording than on that of 1979, when he was in the midst of his artistic crisis and professional switch, his vocal physiognomy alone indicates that he had outgrown the role of Alfredo. The attempt to simulate youthful vitality and exuberance is as futile onstage as it is in bed.

The sound of his voice has lost its dynamic center. Either he sings with a slightly harsh *forte* or *fortissimo,* or he retreats into a whispering crooning with peculiar vocal discolorations, once again primarily at the end of phrases, which he frequently cuts off with an abrupt aspiration. James Levine, whose orchestral blowups occasionally remind one of the excesses of later Karajan recordings, doesn't make his task any easier. He forces the singer into the procrustean bed of the musical bar and deprives him of every opportunity to produce a spontaneous and rhythmically free vocal articulation. When will we ever again hear Alfredo's "Un di felice" or "De' miei bollenti spiriti" with the graceful and tender phrasings of a Fernando de Lucia, "Parigi, o cara" with the hovering and yet full-bodied *pianissimo* and *messa di voce* nuances of a Tito Schipa?

More interesting by far is Pavarotti's interpretation of
Manrico in *Il Trovatore* under the direction of Richard
Bonynge, whose production was received by the press in a
mixed but overwhelmingly critical way. Harold Rosenthal
missed "flesh and blood," and this metaphor shows that the
expectations even of the critics are directed toward a performance with dynamic force and vocal fire—exactly what
Richard Bonynge didn't have to offer. The recording sounds
synthetic; each of the protagonists delivers a role, but there
is little sign of tension between characters or of any dramatic
interaction. Obviously the conductor was more concerned
with creating a retroactive connection to the bel canto tradition and thus about aligning his production with the performance of the young Callas. But that requires a dramatic
talent Joan Sutherland never did possess; her Leonora resembles an official court portrait, with dull vocal colors and
astonishing insecurities in the sustained notes, principally in
the transition position (between E and F).

It may delight the connoisseur to know that Marilyn
Horne actually sings trills in "Stride la vampa" instead of the
usual triplets, but all of that has a decorative effect meant to
brighten up a lean main course. Pavarotti as Manrico: to
borrow a metaphor from Walter Legge, this is a masculine
gazza ladra. Pavarotti himself has repeatedly said that he
studied all available recordings and live tapings prior to the
recording session in order to discover just how his colleagues
mastered the role and cleared its hurdles, each in keeping

with his own talents and capabilities. In the end, he chose Björling as his model.

Who else? The only problem is that Pavarotti's voice never did possess the completely relaxed brilliance that distinguished the Swede's singing. In fact, Björling could actually afford to sing the dark vowels relatively openly in the transition position and could attack them with much greater initial energy. However, Pavarotti's attempt to accentuate the vocal heavyweight in the dramatic scenes—an inclination he was only rarely able to suppress—boomeranged: the exertions once again occasioned that tortured brilliance the listener tolerates but doesn't enjoy.

It's difficult to explain why it took five years before Decca released (or could release) the 1990 recording of *Il Trovatore* produced after performances in Florence. Yet there's nothing new about the fact that Pavarotti recordings have had to wait a long time for their ultimate release to the public. Perhaps Pavarotti perceived the discrepancy between his recorded singing and his live performances.

Ten years earlier, when he sang Manrico under the direction of Richard Bonynge, Pavarotti admitted that his lyrical voice was not the ideal instrument for Manrico. And he added that Jussi Björling—another essentially lyric tenor—had mastered the role. Now, it must be said that the Swede possessed a truly unprecedented volume; he was able to pluck accentuated notes with rigor and sing them with explosive energy. Pavarotti's voice has gained in power and fullness over the years, all the while retaining its lean quality for the most part unchanged. As far as its range is concerned, time has shifted the voice a step and a half. B natural and C have dried up a bit over the decades. What they lack is the *squillo.* Thus, the C's in the *stretta* have a tortured brilliance that produces a rather unpleasant effect, if I may be allowed such a contradiction in terms.

It's all the more disappointing, then, that Pavarotti gives away those passages in which he might have been able to shine in another, lyrically softer way: "Il presagio funesto," once sung by Giovanni Martinelli with aristocratic noblesse, and "Riposa, o madre," once intoned by Caruso with emotional intensity, sound cool and detached coming from Pavarotti. To borrow a phrase from Richard Wagner, what Pavarotti's singing fails to reveal in precisely these instances is "the fundamental essence of human emotion," which, to quote Wagner again, reveals itself "to the ear's eye." That he nevertheless towers head and shoulders above the other members of the ensemble only serves to underscore the woeful dearth of first-class Verdi singers.

It's also symptomatic that one single sour note in a premiere performance of *Don Carlo* at the Teatro alla Scala (1992) not only occasioned excessive protests within the theater, but also spawned headlines all over the world—as well as banal speculations as to whether Pavarotti was losing his voice. This was fame taking its revenge on what had come to be expected perfection. All the while, though, as the videotape shows, the tenor was in good form, either genuinely so or simply because the tape was an edited montage of several performances. Pavarotti sang Carlo with a well-defined, rich tone and sensitive nuances, all of which were once again impaired by the vocal discolorations that have become symptomatic over the past few years and by the strangely aspirated vowels at the end of phrases that terminate in consonants.

Much more irritating than that single sour note, however, was the unbalanced composition of the ensemble. The roles of Elisabetta (Daniela Dessì) and Eboli (Luciana d'Intino) were sung by vocal lightweights who were hardly able to hold their own in the battle against the furiously blaring orchestra. The same is true for the lyric baritone of Paolo Coni, whose vocal means were horribly overextended. This cost the duets and the ensemble scenes all sense of vocal proportion.

It's hard to resist saying at least a few words about the *Aïda* recording under Lorin Maazel: technically perfect but patently indifferent. It was taped live during the December 1985 and January 1986 performances at La Scala, but it was another four years before Pavarotti released it. His reservations are absolutely justified: even if he does sing many selections more beautifully than some of the robust tenors, he is just not cut out for the role of Radames, and it doesn't help much to say by way of excuse that other singers have difficulties with the role as well. But why don't we ever hear anything about the reservations held by the bass Paata Burchuladze? One may recall that he ranked as a great hope a few years ago, but he rumbles in a coarse and uncontrolled manner on this recording. Why don't we hear of baritone Leo Nucci's reservations, whose Rigoletto seems to be sung out and sounds rough and gruff?

Plácido Domingo had just about monopolized the role of Otello for almost two decades by the time Pavarotti sang it in four farewell concert performances in honor of Sir Georg Solti of the Chicago Symphony Orchestra. Critics the world over flew to Chicago and New York to witness the event. Of course, as Friedrich Nietzsche wrote in the fourth of his *Untimely Meditations*, "Richard Wagner in Bayreuth," the measure of an event lies in the greatness of spirit of those who accomplish it as well as in the greatness of spirit of those who experience it.

But how can one experience something that lacks life? A drama like *Otello* without dramatics, without a theatrical atmosphere, without evocative stage sets, without the alternating immersions into love and sorrow, desire and pain—in short, without the excitement and thrills that emanate out of every second of the performances under Ettore Panizza, Arturo Toscanini, or Tullio Serafin? Instead, all we get is a blaring and perfectionistic orchestral brilliance.

Perhaps it was a tactical compliment among rivals when Pavarotti told me that Domingo's portrayal of Otello was "the most brilliant of the century." For whether the soft and darkly melodic voice of the Spaniard, which is not exactly brilliant in pitch, is the proper instrument for the part (even though he has sung it more than two hundred times) is just as doubtful as his representation is contested. The critic Giorgio Gualerzi has politely but emphatically pointed out the limitations of this representation in his historical and comparative study.

Although hesitant at first, Verdi finally did tailor the role to the vocal abilities of Francesco Tamagno. Initially he had been considering a lyric tenor like Angelo Masini for the part. He was hesitant about Tamagno because, as his letters attest, he regarded a *piano* from the native Turin tenor as a "cosa impossibile." These scruples, confirmed by G. B. Shaw's remark about Tamagno's "magnificent screaming" and by William James Henderson's observation that Tamagno delivered his *acuti* with the force of an eight-inch mortar, have become the cornerstone for an all too persistent reputation: Tamagno is still known as the "grand old roarer." All the more remarkable, then, when one hears his voice today: his soft mezza voce in "O muto asil" from *Guglielmo Tell*, or his wonderfully nuanced declamation in the syllabic phrases of "Niun mi tema" ("e tu, come sei pallida," etc.).

Even in the "Esultate," which Verdi conceived with the express wish that it be "an effective phrase" for Tamagno, the composer put less weight on volume than on that particularly penetrating brilliance with which tenor voices with the least trace of baritone timbre are endowed. John Freeman reports that his coach Blanche Marchesi regarded this recording as the most outstanding example of dramatic declamation she had ever heard. Zanelli, Ramon Vinay, Jon Vickers, and even Mario del Monaco agonized over these thirteen bars, be it only at the feared acciaccatura. Why? Because, in keeping with the style of modern tenors, they force the chest voice upward and thus don't treat the transition tones as high notes. In his thought-provoking essay on reception theory, Giorgio Gualerzi points out that Francesco Tamagno's origin was that of a *contraltino*, and that a tradition was turned upside down when the part fell to the *baritenore*: to Zanelli or Vinay.

Francesco Tamagno was Toscanini's first Otello. His second, a half century later, was Ramon Vinay, not because he might have possessed the ideal voice, but because at that time, immediately after the war, there was no other. At the Met, Torsten Ralf sang the part, which had been denied to Lauritz Melchior. Mario del Monaco took it on only in the 1950s. Vinay proved to be less the appropriate singer (his voiced lacked the necessary cutting edge) than an evocative actor. Ramon Vinay was a temporary solution, but an inimitable and in a certain way a commanding one. Nothing attracts an imitator as much as that which is inimitable. The break with tradition, that is, casting the *baritenore* Ramon Venay in the role of Otello, established a new tradition, and not only because most modern tenors, oriented toward the *maniera verista*, sang with a baritone-like forced energy and thus with a constricted pitch.

It's all the more interesting, therefore, so long after Mario del Monaco, Jon Vickers, and Plácido Domingo, to hear a high Italian tenor in the person of Luciano Pavarotti sing the part of Otello. Of course, because of the extremely high position of his voice, Pavarotti lacks the essential sonorous resonance in the many deep passages of the role. Nevertheless, he acquits himself on the whole with remarkable skill and frequently more melodically than does the darker-sounding Domingo, even though he was fighting a bad cold just before the performances.

It would be absurd to expect from Pavarotti's "Esultate" that penetrating, trumpetlike brilliance that Victor Gollancz praised in the singing of Giovanni Zenatello. Pavarotti lends the thirteen bars a truly heroic intensity but is unable even to approximate the expansive phrasing that Tamagno, Zenatello, or de Muro brought to the score. He has an even more difficult time with the slurred lyrical phrases of the love duet. Because the tone doesn't always float on his breath, these phrases sound strained, constricted, and at times muted.

The limitations that become apparent in the second act are predominantly those of the voice: it simply doesn't have enough reserves in volume or enough "blood" in its tone. "What can affect do," Richard Wagner asked in his 1837 essay on dramatic singing, *Der dramatische Gesang*, "if it exceeds one's physical abilities?" In other words, in "Ora per sempre" or in the "sangue" cries, Pavarotti sounds irresolute and bottled up. One notices that he has to control himself when Otello loses control over himself.

The other limitation lies in temperament. Pavarotti never was a singer to abandon himself to a note whose very sound seemed on the verge of bursting into flame, as was Giovanni Martinelli under Ettore Panizza in 1938, to cite another model from the past. This is evident, say, in the final declamatory phrases of "Dio mi potevi scaglier." They never arouse the impression of a man who is beside himself, in a rage of desperate fury. There are other objections to the acoustically unbalanced phrasing choices at the beginning, where Verdi prescribes a *voce soffocata*, or in the syllabic passages of the final monologue. Here, again, melodic passages alternate with flat, acoustically unsupported ones.

Despite all these reservations, however, after so long and so many singers with rough, vocally thick, and coarsely unwieldy voices, a lyric Italian tenor in the person of Luciano Pavarotti has taken on the part of Otello. Most of all, Pavarotti has lent the portrayal a sharper, more immediate profile than did most of his Otello predecessors. What his performance lacks on the whole is a sense of dramatic, of tragic, grandeur, but that is a quality that can only accrue to a singer after long years of practice, after a number of live, onstage performances.

PAVAROTTI AND PUCCINI

Chi son? . . . Son un poeta.

GIACOMO PUCCINI, *La Bohème*, act I

*I*n his brief but impassioned "universal history" of opera, and with the zeal of a music lover objectified in the persona of a charismatic singer, Luca Fontana praises Pavarotti's Rodolfo on the *La Bohème* recording under the direction of Herbert von Karajan. His praise grew out of his conviction that the work had been liberated from the dross of a primitive veristic aesthetic. Among German critical reviews, however, especially those with a Frankfurt school bent, the predominant reaction was that Karajan transposed "the dangerous sophistication of the score to such a height that it took on a new composite dimension."[1]

By means of aesthetic sublimation the conductor, ill disposed toward the crude affectual gestures of verismo, raises a romantically trite story and a sentimental score to a totally different level of reception. He aims the work at a taste that excludes the trivial or at least thinks it can exclude it and yet can't get along without the emotionality. It's the kind of taste that Susan Sontag described as "camp." It's a taste that can delight in the antiquated and the stylized at the same time and that doesn't take the story of those confused bourgeois artists as seriously as it *feels* it when it hears the opera played under the direction of Arturo Toscanini. His hands turn it into a bloody fight to the finish, an existential statement. Toscanini performed the work as if it were a period piece. Karajan transformed it into a sensual play for an audience or for listeners who wanted to be delighted, enchanted, or moved, and thus turned it into an aesthetic tightrope, as Artur Rubinstein once described it when he said there were no boundaries between sweetness and sentimentality. "Yet," he added, "one may not exceed them."

Puccini's Rodolfo is Pavarotti's most evocative portrait ever recorded. Judging by his voice, he sounds like a romantic nobleman, a noble youth burning with passion. His theatrical imagination is most strongly ignited when he has to portray an oaf in a *buffa* scene, a libertine (or even a macho type) in a Verdi opera such as *Rigoletto*, and a sentimental city slicker in one of Puccini's melodramas. This Rodolfo is an acting feat that brings the character visibly to life. What penetration and plasticity of singing, especially in the conversational passages; what effortless brilliance in the brief melodic swoops; what careful phrasing; what eloquence in the aria of the first act; what reserved pathos in the duets and ensembles of the third! In short, a masterful performance that no other tenor has matched, let alone surpassed.

Pavarotti sang the role of Calaf in *Turandot* in 1972 as well. This was a new production admirably conducted by Zubin Mehta. He elaborated the darkly colored combinations of the score, beginning with an often slinky and hesitating melodic stroke, as convincingly as he did the suggestive sensual charms of this strangely exotic music. With the nonintrusive assistance of recording technology, Joan Sutherland and Luciano Pavarotti hold their own with an exemplary projection even in the duet in the second act (toward the end of "In questa reggia" and the riddle scene) against intense orchestral accompaniment. The tenor comes across as unusually reserved and subtle in his aria to Liù, where he strikes a perfect balance between a conversational tone and arioso. Thanks mainly to this reserve, he sounds wonderful. Hardly any other recording is more deserving of its rise in the ranks of the hit parades as Pavarotti's "Nessun dorma."

Madama Butterfly was recorded two years later, in the 1974 reissue under Herbert von Karajan featuring a vocally light Mirella Freni as Cio-Cio-San. The principal aim of this performance, too, was to aesthetically stylize the ambiance with the help of a sensual orchestral allure. Where else can one find such sustained playing? Where too such arbitrary contrasts in the choice of tempi—all the way up to the purely statuesque (in the wedding scene)? Where, finally, such gaudy cinematic effects? What counted as a complete success in the *Bohème* recording here produces a synthetic composite that tends to expose the vocal skills of these singers to a scrutiny they don't quite satisfy. Mirella Freni has to struggle with climactic phrases and just manages to escape, while Pavarotti's constricted singing sounds strained and almost pinched.

One of the clichés of criticism has it that Puccini's operas ought to be entrusted to the batons of none other than the best conductors. The truth of this statement has been demonstrated by Victor de Sabata and Herbert von Karajan in their performances of *Tosca* (not to mention such conductors as Sir Thomas Beecham and Sir John Barbirolli, Arturo Toscanini and, above all, Tullio Serafin). Nicola Rescigno's *Tosca* hardly shines among the Puccini discography, and none of the participating singers—who include Mirella Freni and Sherrill Milnes in addition to Pavarotti—provide a bright spot in the winter of this discontent. It's regrettable enough that Pavarotti's voice at the time of the recording lacked foundation in the deep register, that hardly any of his melodic *piano* passages, let alone a sweet *smorzando*, passed muster, and that the high notes were accompanied by an embarrassing congestion. Even more annoying, however, was what the critic for *High Fidelity* perceived as the "complete lack of dramatic representation," which was replaced by the narcissistic presentation of a singing personality: in other words, by anonymous "tenorizing."[2] To put it yet another way: Pavarotti delivers set pieces from a long since reified arsenal of tenor gestures, with an almost grotesque effect in his eternally sustained "vittoria" in the second act, which, by the way and embarrassingly enough, is not at all victorious from a purely vocal point of view.

PAVAROTTI AND HIS
VERISTIC ROLES

Always sing within your vocal means.

NELLIE MELBA[1]

This is crude, pushy singing, fake-dramatic. He falls into
every trap of the role. His phrasing choices are the obvious
clichés. He resorts to irrelevant bursts of energy to try to fill
out the music. He gets off meaty top notes here and there,
constricted ones at other points. The vibrato turns
tremulous in the middle.

CONRAD L. OSBORNE, "Diary of a CavPag
Madman," *High Fidelity,* June 1979

*C*ritics aren't the only ones to wonder what could have
induced a charming, engaging and popular lyric tenor
with the ideal voice for Edgardo, Elvino, Nemorino, Ernesto, Alfredo, Faust, or Werther to take on roles like that
of Canio and Calaf, Manrico and Radames, Enzo and Andrea Chenier—and to do so at a time when "his upper

range," as the critic and singing coach Conrad L. Osborne noted, was beginning "to lose its juice" as well as what he called its "open-throatedness."² Why, in other words, was Pavarotti tempted to violate the cardinal rule formulated by Nellie Melba (and not only by her) of singing within one's own means and limitations?

One explanation may be that there's an exception to every rule. Alessandro Bonci sang the role of Arturo with a tenor voice that could only be described as lightweight, and as Henderson reports, he hurled his ethereal singing into the furthest recesses of the auditorium. Karl Erb sang Lohengrin with his "boyish" voice, and Alexander Berrsche praised him enthusiastically for doing so. "In those days," Pavarotti adds, "orchestras had fewer members and conductors were not yet afraid of playing softly." To cite a few younger and perhaps the most significant examples: the young Jussi Björling, like Pavarotti a lyric tenor as far as his vocal talents were concerned, also sang *spinto* roles at the Met, including Manrico, Cavaradossi, Turriddu, Des Grieux, and Don Carlo. But he didn't sing them any differently than he did his lyric roles; in other words, he didn't add volume that could be attained only with strain and physical exertion. Even Carlo Bergonzi knew how to maneuver a none too voluminous and not very penetrating voice through difficult parts with technical skill and an impressive sense for dramatic effect. The baritone Victor Maurel, so highly prized by Verdi, the first Iago as well as the first Falstaff, once said that the public soon grows tired of a singer who sings loudly all the time. To his mind, a dynamic delivery was much more effective than a sustained melodic projection.

This is much more important for the lyric than for the dramatic tenor. Pavarotti never did possess the means to sustain an unflagging brilliance and forceful projection in his roles as Radames, Andrea Chenier, or Canio as did Mario del Monaco or even Franco Corelli, for example. In other words, he ought to have tried to find his own vocal dramaturgy for the difficult roles. This has absolutely nothing to do with that type of compensatory acting that lets the singer disregard such technical details as the execution of ornamentations, trills, and coloratura. It's simply a fact that *leggiero* tenors like Tito Schipa or Ferruccio Tagliavini have to design their parts differently than singers who are endowed with more richly melodic means. In our day Nicolai Gedda and Alfredo Kraus were masters of this vocal economy.

The picture that graces both the 1978 album covers as well as the promotional pages for the *CavPag* recording can be taken as a response to the question why Pavarotti sang his first naturalistic, or veristic, parts. The picture shows him wearing the costume of the drum-beating Pagliaccio—Caruso's costume. It thus shows him appropriating not only Caruso's musical but his societal role as well. It shows him trying to revive the old myth and to become the tenor of tenors: the symbol of the tenor, pure and simple.

It's more than irritating when a singer who actually did

make a sensitive and romantic youth out of Puccini's Rodolfo under the direction of Herbert von Karajan employs gestures in the *Pagliacci* recording that the fathers of the (vocal) ragbag had already used and abused. Like Benjamino Gigli and Mario del Monaco, who transformed inner emotionality into weepy sentimentality, Pavarotti sobs his way into the sequel to Canio's *lamento* and abandons himself to that false theatrical howl that Thomas Mann so aptly described in his *Mario and the Magician* as the "primordial shriek of heroic anguish." Pavarotti's presentation strikes the listener as an unsuccessfully integrated adaptation of more or less familiar effects that echo through his performance. He summons up all his vocal energies for some of the exposed passages, such as the invitation to the peasants "a ventitrè ore" or the climactic phrase in "Recitar" leading up to the A. Yet the careful and critical listener can hear what these efforts cost him in the dull, pale tones of the middle register, which simply rebel against high pressure. A voice in this register has fullness, warmth, and sonority only when the singing is completely uninhibited and possesses a *piano* resonance. Despite all the idiosyncrasies Mario del Monaco and Franco Corelli displayed in their singing that previously elicited my disapproval, I must say that, upon recent relistenings to their recordings, I have sincerely regretted my remarks, for they are not as bad as I once thought they were.

It remains a puzzle why a lyric tenor in the role of Turriddu should sing "O Lola" the way Otello sings his "Ora per sempre addio," namely, loudly and aggressively. Actually, it's no puzzle at all—the whole piece is situated in the critical upper middle register and can be kept under control only when the *piano* functionings of the voice are in good working order. In coming to terms with Julia Varady's Santuzza, who is surely no Sicilian as far as her voice and temperament are concerned, Pavarotti carries more than the costume of the role, and even the *brindisi* and the "Addìo alla Madre" turn out better.

The third role in his veristic repertoire was that of Enzo in Amilcare Ponchielli's *La Gioconda*, which he also sang at the opening of the 1979–80 season in San Francisco. As far as melodic richness, dramatic coherence, and theatrical effect are concerned, Ponchielli's opera is a masterpiece. That it's relatively unknown may perhaps be due to the difficulty of casting six parts with top singers and of finding a Callas or a vocal beauty like Milanov for the title role. Or a Ponselle. Or Gianina Arangi-Lombardi, who is not yet a household name. To mention a few others in this context (and the other roles as well): Ebe Stignani and Irene Minghini-Cataneo as Laura; Caruso, the young Gigli, Jussi Björling and, for stylistic reasons, Fernando de Lucia as Enzo, and after the war surely Richard Tucker and Carlo Bergonzi; Titta Ruffo, Riccardo Stracciari, Giuseppe de Luca, and Pasquale Amato as Barnaba, and later Leonard Warren and Robert Merrill; and finally Tancredi Pasero, Ezio Pinza, or Cesare Siepi as Alvise.

This list is meant to serve as nothing more than a casting guide, for Ponchielli's opera needs strong, healthy voices with dramatic expression. In saying that, however, I am not referring to fullness or penetrating power, but rather to a theatrical energy coupled with vocal colors and shadings. Neither Montserrat Caballé (in the title role) nor Agnes Baltsa possess the means for their roles. In fact, the latter has been miscast in dramatic roles for years now because of a lack of suitable singers. Alan Blyth writes that Pavarotti's "Enzo makes a forceful entrance at 'Assassin.'"[3] One wonders whether that's meant as a euphemism for mere strain, for a flat, harsh, and in the lower register, hollow sound? When a singer brightens the open vowels for dramatic effect, it's always a sign of vocal stress, and there is only one word for the sudden and explosive termination of consonants: *Mummenschanz*, or masquerading.

How did William James Henderson once describe Caruso's interpretation of "Cielo e mar"? As one of the loftiest flights of his lyric genius. As the imaginative, poetic rendition of a sensuous hymn. One must measure Pavarotti not against Caruso, but against the Pavarotti of the 1969–70 recital mentioned above. There he was a young and careful tenor in control of his rhythm and his acoustic shadings. If we make this comparison, we're moved to cry out "ohimè" or "perduto" with Italian gusto, and this all the more desperately when confronted with the completely sung-out voice of Nicolai Ghiaurov in the role of Alvise.

A similar situation surrounds the title role in Arrigo Boito's opera *Mefistofele*. Boito is a relative unknown. An

Italian (some say a French) composer and the *Faust* theme?
For German critics there is only one word, and a crushing
one at that, that seems to deliver the appropriate aesthetic
verdict of such a work: Goethe. The prelude to the work is
devoted to Boito's infernal hero, and in portraying him,
Ghiaurov, whom Steane optimistically prophesied as the
living legacy of "the grand tradition" in his 1970 book, has
more hot air to offer than controlled singing. The low register sounds dull, hoarse, and breathy. The singer tries to
compensate for this defect with a type of overpressure in the
middle and upper registers and a ghastly vocal masquerade.
This is all the more regrettable since Pavarotti obviously has
some respect for Faust. In a performance excellently conducted by Oliviero de Fabritiis, he sings the role in a more
reserved and more poetic manner than he has done in almost
all his other roles during the last ten years.

Like Ponchielli's *La Gioconda*, Umberto Giordano's *Andrea Chenier* is also a gloriously bridled warhorse for any
company able to provide a superb cast, and not one big name
is missing from the phalanx of singers who have sung the
part of this revolutionary poet. The singer in the premiere
performance was Giuseppe Borgatti, the wonderful tenor of
Toscanini's first Italian productions of Wagner, and he was
followed by Francesco Tamagno and Giovanni Zenatello,
Enrico Caruso and Benjamino Gigli, Giovanni Martinelli
and Giacomo Lauri-Volpi. The postwar singers included
Mario del Monaco and Franco Corelli, followed most re-

cently by Plácido Domingo and Luciano Pavarotti. The latter sang three of Chenier's scenes during his recital of veristic
arias with "possibly the most wonderful voice, objectively
considered, of any Chenier on record" (William Mann).4
Unfortunately, he spoiled his performance by showing off his
top notes and by "tirading" (Mann), which is to say, exagger-
ating the rhetorical aspects of the selections.

In his column "The Gramophone and the Voice," John
Steane wrote enthusiastically about these excerpts from
Chenier and later about Pavarotti on the complete recording.
This is surprising, especially when one considers the other
interpreters of the role. Rhetorical emphasis—say, in the
middle part of "Un dì all'azzro spazio"—has to come through
in the singing, and not everyone can be as assertive *fortissimo
con somma passione* the way Martinelli or Mario del Monaco
once could. The latter was the focal point of a fascinatingly
theatrical performance conducted by Gianandrea Gavazzeni
with Renata Tebaldi (whose singing was effective but not
terribly nuanced) and Ettore Bastianini. A better baritone or
tenor have hardly been recorded, and surely none more suggestive. Evocative and carefree at the same time is Franco
Corelli's Chenier, who acts like a buccaneer, as it were, an
Errol Flynn of song, but for all that he at least contributes a
voice that smacks of raw beef.

Plácido Domingo sang the title role in the captivating 1977
performance under James Levine, and he has rarely given a
more convincing interpretation than on this album. The

flamboyance of veristic singing corresponds to his voice better than it does to Pavarotti's, even though the latter is
surrounded by excellent *comprimarii* (Christa Ludwig, Kathleen Kuhlmann, Astrid Varnay, Tom Krause, Piero de
Palma) in the competently conducted recording under Riccardo Chailly. Unfortunately, the other main roles sung by
Montserrat Caballé and Leo Nucci were less appropriately
cast. Gregory Sandow published his review in *High Fidelity*:
"Luciano Pavarotti sounds as though he were not involved in
the drama at all. Despite his efforts to salvage his artistic
integrity above his career as an entertainer, he gives the
impression of having forgotten what differentiates an Italian tenor role from that of others. But he actually did regain
his vocal freedom. . . . His singing beams, it's totally pli-
able, worlds better than in the three excerpts on his recital
recording."[5]

At least it shows a striving for form and a tempered pathos
more appropriate to the voice as an instrument than excesses
à la Gigli, who was a brilliant interpreter of the role in his
own way.

PAVAROTTI THE MAN, OR
HIS PACKAGING

The high C is the keynote of this selection of operatic scenes.

Inscription on an album cover

*T*empting but obsolete are all efforts to formulate lengthy culture-critical commentaries about recital recordings, to criticize the fetishization of high notes, to bemoan the public's waning ability to listen with discrimination. Ever since the invention of the sound recording, this technical form of reproduction has served both God and mammon; it has preserved music while simultaneously promoting the singing star.

The only thing that matters in all of this is whether or not these stars have placed themselves in the service of music. There's a big difference between, on the one hand, Maria Callas carefully portraying Puccini's *femmes fragiles* in the recital hall or her developing a concept of subtle verismo singing as the sum total of her artistic career, and, on the other hand, dishing up the same repertoire again and again for the sole purpose of making a splash on the charts.

Those even slightly familiar with Pavarotti's recordings have no easy task in classifying and integrating them into some kind of meaningful whole: they range from *Tutto Pavarotti* or *The Essential Pavarotti* to *Big P.* and *Pavarotti Anniversary*, from *Pavarotti Sings Verdi* and *Pavarotti Sings Donizetti* to *Mattinata* and *Volare*, from *Primo Tenore* and *Pavarotti in Albert Hall* to *Pavarotti in Concert* and *Favorite Italian Songs*, from *Yes, Giorgio* to *The Great Voices of the Arena in Verona*—and one could probably find a few additional titles if one tried.

Bravo, Pavarotti! (another natural for a title!) Bravissimo! (that, too, maybe?) In the meantime, into this global *bravissimo* has been packed everything a microphone was able to catch: concerts from Modena and Verona with this or that diva, sometimes successful and more often not so successful. He is ebullience personified, and even if not always that of melodious sound, he still ranks as the incarnation of "opera bigwigs" in the double sense of the word that Klaus Umbach described in his *Geldscheinsonate*.

"Don't you know that a tenor is not a denizen of this world, his is a world in himself," Hector Berlioz once wrote. A century and a half later Luciano Pavarotti has transformed the tenor into its age-appropriate version: into a star, who is unquestionably an integral part of this world. Stendhal feared that "in the twentieth century people will be talking only about politics," unaware that in a society characterized by the democratic leveling of all people and by the banalization of aesthetics everything and everyone has become equivalent and thus no longer possessing of any particular individual consequence.

In the person of "Grandissimo Pavarotti" the tenor has metamorphosed into a *Gesamtkunstwerk*, a media phenomenon, a share of stock. He embodies the prototype of the tenor and is at the same time its parody. Pavarotti was a brilliant singer and still is a good one; all the same, he's the one who determines the repeal and annullment of all standards. It's not only hard to understand but also insufferable that Pavarotti should stuff his audience with the same sweets that Benjamino Gigli used to serve: "Mamma." What once stood in the service of seduction as well as of political infantilization and demagogic consolation today serves to trivialize the aesthetic.

Works of art are destroyed when aesthetic discrimination is destroyed. Such a sense for art, however, is not born of itself. It has to be evoked and cultivated by the artist. Many artists are inclined to give the public only what it wants. Few possess the energy to demand of the public what the work of art requires.

We need no further commentary, just a brief, melancholy conclusion. It comes from an opera whose tenor hero was not heroic enough for a tenor and who lived in the antiquated tradition of the good old days. The piece is called *Così fan tutte*.

DISCOGRAPHY

OPERAS

BELLINI

Beatrice di Tenda
Sutherland/Pavarotti/Veasey
Ambrosian Opera Chorus
London Symphony
Orchestra
Richard Bonynge. 1966
Decca 433 706-2

Norma
Sutherland/Caballé/Pavarotti/
Ramey
Orchestra and Chorus of the
Welsh National Opera
Richard Bonynge. 1984
414 476-2
Decca (3 CDs) DDD

I Puritani
Sutherland/Pavarotti/
Cappuccilli/Ghiaurov
London Symphony
Orchestra
Richard Bonynge. 1973
417 588-2
Decca (3 CDs) ADD

La Sonnambula
Sutherland/Pavarotti/
Ghiaurov
National Philharmonic
Orchestra
Richard Bonynge. 1980
417 424-2
Decca (2 CDs) DDD

BOITO
Mefistofele
Ghiaurov/Pavarotti/Freni/
Caballé
National Philharmonic
Orchestra
Oliviero de Fabritiis. 1980/82
410 175-2
Decca (3 CDs) DDD

DONIZETTI
Anna Bolena
Pavarotti/Sutherland/Ramey/
Hadley/Mentzer
Orchestra and Chorus of the
Welsh National Opera
Richard Bonynge
421 096-2
Decca (3 CDs) DDD

L'Elisir d'Amore
Battle/Pavarotti/Nucci/Dara/
Upshaw
Choir and Orchestra of the
Metropolitan Opera
James Levine
DG 429 744-2

L'Elisir d'Amore
Sutherland/Pavarotti/Cossa/
 Malas
Ambrosian Opera Chorus
English Chamber Orchestra
Richard Bonynge. 1970
414 461-2
Decca (2 CDs) ADD

La Favorita
Cosotto/Pavarotti/Bacquier/
 Ghiaurov
Orchestra e Coro del Teatro
 Comunale di Bologna
Richard Bonynge
430 038-2
Decca (3 CDs) ADD

La Fille du Régiment
Sutherland/Pavarotti/Malas/
 Sinclair
Orchestra and Chorus of the
 Royal Opera House,
 Covent Garden
Richard Bonynge. 1967
414 520-2
Decca (2 CDs) ADD

Lucia di Lammermoor
Scotto/Manganotto/Pavarotti/
 Stasto
Choir and Orchestra of the
 RAI, Turin
Molinari Pradelli. 1994
Zyx CLS 4604

Lucia di Lammermoor
Sutherland/Milnes/Pavarotti/
 Ghiaurov
Orchestra and Chorus of the
 Royal Opera House,
 Covent Garden
Richard Bonynge. 1971
410 193-2
Decca (3 CDs) ADD

Maria Stuarda
Sutherland/Tourangeau/
 Pavarotti/Morris/Soyer
Orchestra e Coro del Teatro
 Comunale di Bologna
Richard Bonynge. 1974/75
425 410-2
Decca (2 CDs) ADD

Requiem
Bruson Cortez/Pavarotti
Orchestra e Coro Ente
 Lirico Arena di Verona
D. Fackler. 1980/92
425 013-2
Decca/ASPEKTE

Donizetti Arias
*La Fille du Régiment, L'Elisir
 d'Amore, La Favorita, Il
 Duca d'Alba, Dom
 Sébastien, Don Pasquale,
 Maria Stuarda, Lucia di
 Lammermoor*
Luciano Pavarotti
with various orchestras and
 conductors
417 638-2
Decca ADD

DISCOGRAPHY

Verdi and Donizetti
Arias from Luisa Miller,
  Macbeth, Un Ballo in
  Maschera, La Favorita,
  Lucia di Lammermoor, etc.
421 304-2
Decca ADD

GIORDANO
Andrea Chenier
Pavarotti/Caballé/Nucci
National Philharmonic
  Orchestra, London
Riccardo Chailly. 1983/84
410 117-2
Decca (2 CDs) DDD

LEONCAVALLO
Pagliacci
Freni/Pavarotti/Saccomani/
  Wixell
National Philharmonic
  Orchestra, London.
Giuseppe Patané. 1977
421 870-2
Decca (2 CDs) ADD
(+ Mascagni, *Cavalleria
  Rusticana*)

I Pagliacci
Dessi/Pavarotti/Pons/Conti/
  Gavazzi
Philadelphia Orchestra
Riccardo Muti. 1992/93
Ph 434 431-2

MASCAGNI
L'Amico Fritz
Freni/Pavarotti/Sardinero/
  Major/others
Orchestra and Chorus of
  the Royal Opera House,
  Covent Garden
Gianandrea Gavazzeni.
  1969/87
EMI CDS 7 47905 8

Cavalleria Rusticana
Varady/Pavarotti/Cappuccilli
National Philharmonic
  Orchestra, London
Gianandrea Gavazzeni. 1976
414 590-2
Decca (2 CDs) ADD
(FRG 8 35 445 ZA)
(+ Leoncavallo, *Pagliacci*)

MOZART
Idomeneo
Pavarotti/Popp/Baltsa/
  Gruberova/Nucci
Wiener Staatsopernchor
Wiener Philharmoniker
Sir John Pritchard. 1983
411 805-2
Decca (3 CDs) DDD

PONCHIELLI
La Gioconda
Caballé/Pavarotti/Baltsa/
  Milnes/Ghiaurov
National Philharmonic
  Orchestra, London
Bruno Bartoletti. 1980
414 349-2
Decca (3 CDs) DDD

PUCCINI
La Bohème
Freni/Pavarotti/Ghiaurov
Berliner Philharmoniker
Herbert von Karajan. 1972
421 049-2
Decca (2 CDs) ADD

La Bohème
Freni/Rocco/Pavarotti/Orazi/
Polo
Choir and Orchestra of the
Teatro Comunale Modena
Leone Magiera
Zyx CLS 4601

Madama Butterfly
Freni/Pavarotti/Ludwig
Kerns
Wiener Philharmoniker
Herbert von Karajan. 1974
417 577-2
Decca (3 CDs) ADD

Manon Lescaut
Freni/Pavarotti/Croft/Bartoli/
Taddei/Vargas
Chorus and Orchestra of the
Metropolitan Opera
James Levine. 1992
Decca 440 200-2

Tosca
Freni/Pavarotti/Milnes
National Philharmonic
Orchestra, London
Nicola Rescigno. 1978
414 036-2
Decca (2 CDs) ADD

Turandot
Sutherland/Pavarotti/Caballé/
Ghiaurov
London Philharmonic
Orchestra
Zubin Mehta. 1972
414 274-2
Decca (2 CDs) ADD

ROSSINI
Guglielmo Tell
Pavarotti/Freni/Milnes
National Philharmonic
Orchestra, London
Riccardo Chailly. 1978/79
417 154-2
Decca (4 CDs) ADD

Petite Messe Solennelle
Freni/Pavarotti/Valentini/
Raimondi
Coro Polifonico del Teatro
alla Scala
Romano Gandolfi. 1977
SDD 567/8 EC
Decca 421 645-2

Stabat Mater
Lorengar/Minton/Pavarotti/
Sotin
London Symphony
Orchestra and Chorus
István Kertész. 1971
417 766-2
Decca ADD

RICHARD STRAUSS
Der Rosenkavalier
Pavarotti/Crespin/Jungwirth/
   Minton
Wiener Philharmoniker
Sir Georg Solti
417 493-2
Decca (3 CDs) ADD

VERDI
Aïda
Chiara/Dimitrova/Pavarotti/
   Nucci/Burchuladze
Orchestra e Coro del Teatro
   alla Scala
Lorin Maazel. 1972/83
417 439-2
Decca (3 CDs) DDD

Un Ballo in Maschera
Tebaldi/Milnes/Resnik/
   Pavarotti/Donath
Coro e Orchestra
   dell'Accademia di Santa
   Cecilia, Rome
Bruno Bartoletti. 1970/93
SET 484/6 GF
Decca 440 012-2

Un Ballo in Maschera
Pavarotti/M. Price/Bruson
National Philharmonic
   Orchestra, London
Sir Georg Solti. 1982/83
410 210-2
Decca (2 CDs) DDD

Ernani
Sutherland/Pavarotti/Nucci/
   Burchuladze
Orchestra and Chorus of the
   Welsh National Opera
Richard Bonynge
421 412-2
Decca (3 CDs) DDD

Luisa Miller
Caballé/Pavarotti/Milnes
National Philharmonic
   Orchestra, London
Peter Maag. 1975
417 420-2
Decca (2 CDs) ADD

Macbeth
Souliotis/Fischer-Dieskau/
   Pavarotti/Ghiaurov
Ambrosian Opera Chorus
London Philharmonic
   Orchestra
Lamberto Gardelli. 1971
SET 510/2 GF
Decca 440 048-2

Otello
Kanawa/Pavarotti/Nucci
Chicago Symphony
   Orchestra
Sir Georg Solti. 1991
Decca 433 669-2

Requiem
Sutherland/Horne/Pavarotti/
Talvela
Wiener Philharmoniker
Sir Georg Solti. 1967
411 944-2
Decca (2 CDs) ADD

Messa da Requiem
Studer/Zajic/Pavarotti/Ramey
Coro e Orchestra del Teatro
alla Scala
Riccardo Muti. 1987/92
EMI 667 7 749 390 2

Rigoletto
Anderson/Pavarotti/Nucci/
Ghiaurov/Verrett
Orchestra e Coro del Teatro
Comunale di Bologna
Riccardo Chailly. 1989
425 864-2
London (2 CDs) DDD

Rigoletto
Sutherland/Pavarotti/Milnes/
Talvela
London Symphony
Orchestra
Richard Bonynge. 1971
414 269-2
Decca (2 CDs) ADD
Scenes and Arias
421 303-2 D A
Decca ADD

La Traviata
Studer/Pavarotti/White/Kelly/
Pons
Chorus and Orchestra of the
Metropolitan Opera
James Levine. 1992
DG436 797-2

La Traviata
Sutherland/Pavarotti/
Manuguerra
National Philharmonic
Orchestra, London
Richard Bonynge. 1979
430 491-2
Decca (3 CDs) DDD
Highlights
400 057-2 D H
Decca DDD

Il Trovatore
Banaudi/Pavarotti/Nucci/
Verrett
Choir and Orchestra of the
Maggio Musicale
Fiorentino
Zubin Mehta. 1995
Decca 430 694-2

Il Trovatore
Sutherland/Horne/Pavarotti
National Philharmonic
Orchestra, London
Richard Bonynge. 1976
417 137-2
Decca (2 CDs) ADD
Scenes and Arias
421 310-2
Decca ADD

Verdi Arias
Aïda, Rigoletto, Il Trovatore,
  Un Ballo in Maschera, La
  Traviata, etc.
Luciano Pavarotti
with various orchestras and
  conductors
417 570-2
Decca DDD/ADD

*R*ECITALS AND
*C*ONCERTS

LUCIANO PAVAROTTI
Anniversary Album
La Bohème, Andrea Chenier,
  La Traviata, Pagliacci, Un
  Ballo in Maschera,
  Mefistofele, Guglielmo Tell,
  Tosca, Cavalleria Rusticana
Luciano Pavarotti
with various orchestras and
  conductors
417 362-2
Decca DDD/ADD

Donizetti Arias
La Fille du Régiment, L'Elisir
  d'Amore, La Favorita, Il
  Duca d'Alba, Dom
  Sébastien, Don Pasquale,
  Maria Stuarda, Lucia di
  Lammermoor
Luciano Pavarotti
with various orchestras and
  conductors
417 638-2
Decca ADD

The Essential Pavarotti
Rigoletto, La Bohème, Tosca,
  Turandot, L'Elisir
  d'Amore, "Caruso,"
  "Mattinata," "Volare," "O
  sole mio," etc.
Luciano Pavarotti
430 210-2
Decca AAD/ADD/DDD

The Essential Pavarotti II
Rigoletto, Fedora, Aïda,
  Werther, songs
Decca 430 470-2

Favorite Tenor Arias
Pagliacci, Carmen, La
  Bohème, Rigoletto, Tosca,
  Faust, Turandot, Il
  Trovatore
Luciano Pavarotti
with various orchestras and
  conductors
400 053-2
Decca ADD

Gala Concert at the Royal
  Albert Hall
Tosca, Macbeth, I Lombardi,
  Luisa Miller, Turandot, etc.
Luciano Pavarotti
Royal Philharmonic
  Orchestra
Kurt Herbert Adler
430 716-2
Decca DDD

King of the High C
Arias from *The Daughter of
the Regiment, Favorita,
Trovatore, Puritani,
Bohème*
Decca 421 326-2

My Heart's Delight
Live Recital in Piazza
Grande, Modena,
September 1993 with
Nuccia Forile, soprano
Royal Philharmonic
Orchestra, London
Maurizio Benini
Decca 443 260-2

Pavarotti at Carnegie Hall
Scarlatti, Schubert, Verdi
Liszt, Tosti, Donizetti,
Mascagni, et al.
Luciano Pavarotti
John Wustman, piano
421 526-2
Decca DDD

Pavarotti in Concert
Songs by Handel, Bellini,
Rossini, Respighi, Tosti,
et al.
Luciano Pavarotti
Orchestra del Teatro
Comunale di Bologna
Richard Bonynge
425 037-2
Decca ADD

Pavarotti in Central Park
Arias from *Lucia di
Lammermoor, Tosca,
Werther, Luisa Miller*, etc.
(live, 1993)
Andrea Griminelli, flute
New York Philharmonic
Leone Magiera
Decca 444 450-2

Pavarotti in Hyde Park
Arias from *L'Africana, Luisa
Miller, Tosca, Turandot*,
"Mamma," "O sole mio,"
etc.
Philharmonia Orchestra,
London
Leone Magiera
Decca 436 320-2

Tutto Pavarotti
"Caruso," "O sole mio,"
"Passione," "Mamma," "O
Holy Night," "Celeste
Aïda," "Una furtiva
lagrima," "Di quella pira,"
"La donna è mobile,"
"M'appari," "O paradiso,"
"Vesti la giubba," "Che
gelida manina," etc.
Luciano Pavarotti
425 681-2
Decca DDD/ADD

DISCOGRAPHY

Verdi Arias
Aïda, Rigoletto, Il Trovatore,
Un Ballo in Maschera, La
Traviata, etc.
Luciano Pavarotti
with various orchestras and
conductors
417 570-2
Decca DDD/ADD

Verismo Arias
Mefistofele, Andrea Chenier,
Manon Lescaut, etc.
Luciano Pavarotti
National Philharmonic
Orchestra
Oliviero de Fabritiis/
Riccardo Chailly
440 180-2
Decca DDD

PAVAROTTI / FRENI
Pavarotti/Freni "Live"
La Traviata, Werther, La
Gioconda, L'Amico Fritz,
L'Elisir d'Amore, I Vespri
Siciliani, L'Africana, etc.
Mirella Freni/Luciano
Pavarotti
Orchestra dell' Ater
Leone Magiera
421 862-2
Decca ADD

Pavarotti/Freni "Live"
Arias from *La Traviata,*
Aïda, Otello, Turandot,
Tosca, etc.
Various orchestras and
conductors
Decca 443 018-2

Arias and Duets
La Bohème, Tosca, Guglielmo
Tell, Mefistofele
Mirella Freni/Luciano
Pavarotti
421 878-2
Decca ADD/DDD

PAVAROTTI/RICCIARELLI
Pavarotti/Ricciarelli "Live"
La Traviata, Aïda, Macbeth,
La Forza del Destino, I
Lombardi, Il Corsaro,
Falstaff, Otello
Katia Ricciarelli/Luciano
Pavarotti
Orchestra del Teatro Regio
di Palma
Giuseppe Patanè
421 863-2
Decca ADD

*Pavarotti and Levine in
Recital*
Arias and Songs by Mozart,
Rossini, Bellini, Verdi,
Massenet, Respighi,
Puccini, et al.
Luciano Pavarotti
James Levine, piano
VHS (PAL): 071 119-3
Laser Disc (PAL: 1 disc/2
sides): 071 119-1
Decca DDD

CARRERAS/DOMINGO/
PAVAROTTI
In Concert
Recorded "Live" in Rome,
7 July 1990
Arias and songs with
specially arranged medley
José Carreras/Plácido
Domingo/Luciano
Pavarotti
Orchestra del Maggio
Musicale Fiorentino e
Orchestra del Teatro
dell'Opera di Roma
Zubin Mehta
CD/LP/MC: 430 433-2/-1/-4
VHS (PAL): 071 123-3
Laser Disc (PAL: 1 disc/2
sides): 430 433-2
Decca DDD

*Carreras-Domingo-Pavarotti
with Mehta. The Three
Tenors in Concert, "Live"
from Dodger Stadium, Los
Angeles, June 1994*
Los Angeles Philharmonic
Orchestra, Music Center
Opera Chorus
Zubin Mehta
Decca 4509 98200-2

SUTHERLAND/HORNE/
PAVAROTTI
*Live from Lincoln Center
Ernani, Norma, La Gioconda,
Otello, Il Trovatore*
Joan Sutherland/Marilyn
Horne/Luciano Pavarotti
New York City Opera
Orchestra
Richard Bonynge
417 587-2
Decca DDD

SUTHERLAND/PAVAROTTI
*Operatic Duets
La Traviata, Aïda, Otello,* etc.
Joan Sutherland/Luciano
Pavarotti
National Philharmonic
Orchestra
Richard Bonynge
400 058-2
Decca ADD

Operatic Duets
Lucia di Lammermoor,
  Rigoletto, L'Elisir d'Amore,
  Maria Stuarda, La Fille du
  Régiment, I Puritani
Joan Sutherland/Luciano
  Pavarotti
with various orchestras and
  conductors
Richard Bonynge
421 894-2
Decca ADD

Primo Tenore
Guglielmo Tell, I Puritani,
  Don Pasquale, Mefistofele,
  Il Trovatore, La Gioconda,
  etc.
Luciano Pavarotti
Wiener Opernorchester und
  -chor
New Philharmonia Orchestra
417 713-2
Decca ADD

The Pavarotti Edition
Arias
Special boxed set containing
  4 CDs: Donizetti arias,
  Verdi arias, and operatic
  arias by other composers
Luciano Pavarotti
421 122-2
Decca (4 CDs) DDD/ADD

Greatest Hits
Turandot, Tosca, Carmen,
  Rigoletto, Aïda, Il
  Trovatore, Faust, etc.
Luciano Pavarotti
with various orchestras and
  conductors
417 011-2
Decca (2 CDs) ADD

Mamma
16 Popular Italian Songs
Luciano Pavarotti
Henry Mancini
411 959-2
Decca DDD

O sole mio
Favorite Neapolitan Songs
Luciano Pavarotti
410 015-2
Decca ADD

O Holy Night
Popular Christmas Songs
"Cantique de Noël,"
  "Panis Angelicus," "Ave
  Maria," etc.
Luciano Pavarotti
National Philharmonic
  Orchestra
Kurt Herbert Adler
433 710-2
Decca ADD

Passione
"Passione," "Era de
  Maggio," "Fenesta che
  Lucive," "Chiove,"
  "Dicitencello Vuie," "La
  Palummella," "Voce'e
  notte," etc.
Luciano Pavarotti
Orchestra del Teatro
  Comunale di Bologna
Giancarlo Chiaramello
417 117-2
Decca DDD

Volare
Popular Italian Songs
Luciano Pavarotti
Henry Mancini
421 052-2
Decca DDD

The Pavarotti Edition
Songs
Special boxed set containing
  4 CDs: "Mamma,"
  "O sole mio," "Mattinata,"
  and "Passione"
Luciano Pavarotti
421 121-2
Decca (4 CDs) DDD/ADD
(FRG 8 35 771 ZC)

Mattinata
Italian songs by Tosti,
  Rossini, Gluck, Donizetti,
  Bellini, Giordani, et al.
Luciano Pavarotti
Philharmonia Orchestra
Piero Gamba
417 796-2
Decca ADD

PAVAROTTI ON VIDEO

Il Trovatore
Marlon/Pavarotti/Zajic/
 Milnes
Chorus and Orchestra of the
 Metropolitan Opera
James Levine
DG VHS: PAL 072 413-3

MISCELLANY
In Concert in China
Exhibition Hall Theatre,
 Peking, 1986 (1989)
Arias from *Rigoletto,
Pagliacci, Turandot,* et al.
Orchestra and Chorus of the
 Municipal Opera, Genoa
Pickwick Video RPT 2010

I grandi della lirica
Operas by Bellini, Puccini,
 Leoncavallo, et al.
Biographia, prodotto della
 RAI
Edizione Center TV, Milano

*Great Moments: Highlights
from Paravotti in Hyde Park*
Dec VHS 071 191-3

My Heart's Delight
Twenty arias, songs, and
 duets by Puccini,
 Mascagni, Lehár, Verdi,
 Bizet, et al.
Pavarotti/Focile
Royal Philharmonic
 Orchestra, London
Maurizio Benini
Dec VHS 071 119-3

My Heart's Delight
See CD listing in
 Discography
Dec VHS 071 164-3

Nessun Dorma
May 1990
Arias from *L'Elixir d'Amore,
Lucia di Lammermoor,
Lombardi, Werther,
Pagliacci, Butterfly,* etc.
A. Griminelli, flute
Chamber Orchestra of
 Bologna
Leone Magiera
Collecton Series, Col 1004

Pavarotti and Friends
See CD listing in
 Discography
Dec VHS 071 160-3

Pavarotti and Friends, 2
With Adams/Bocelli/
 Georgia/Gustafson/et al.
"Live" from the Parco Novi
 Sad, Modena. 1994
Dec VHS 071 185-3

*Pavarotti and Levine (piano)
in Recital.*
Arias and songs by Mozart,
 Rossini, Bellini, Verdi,
 Massenet, Respighi, et al.
Dec VHS 017 119-3

Pavarotti in Central Park
See CD listing in
   Discography
Dec VHS 071 180-3

Pavarotti in Hyde Park
See CD listing in
   Discography
Dec VHS 071 150-3

30th Anniversary Gala Concert
"Live" from Teatro Valli,
   Reggio, 1991
Arias and duets by Puccini,
   Donizetti, Verdi, et al.
Orchestra del Teatro
   Comunale di Bologna
Magiera Benini
Dec VHS 071 140-3

NOTES

PREFACE

1. Martin Mayer, *Grandissimo Pavarotti: A Celebration of the Career of the World's Greatest Tenor on the Silver Anniversary of His Debut.* New York, 1986.

VOX POPULI

1. Klaus Umbach, *Geldscheinsonate: Das Millionenspiel mit der Klassik* (Frankfurt am Main, 1990), p. 271. [This book is not available in English translation; the title of the chapter cited is "Oper dicke: Luciano Pavarotti." Mr. Umbach is fond of puns; the title of his book is a play on Beethoven's "Mondscheinsonate," *Geldschein* being the German word for "banknote." *Trans.*]
2. "Opera's Golden Tenor," *Time*, September 24, 1979.
3. Umbach, *Geldscheinsonate*, p. 273.
4. *Time*, September 24, 1979.

OF KINGS AND POTENTATES

1. Quoted in Mayer, *Grandissimo Pavarotti*, p. 118.
2. Peter Sloterdijk, *Critique of Cynical Reason*, trans. Michael Eldred (Minneapolis, 1987), p. 316.
3. Ibid.
4. See Hubert Saal, "The Great Pavarotti," *Newsweek*, March 15, 1976.
5. Quoted in Horowitz, *Understanding Toscanini* (New York, 1987), p. 409.
6. Ibid.
7. Quoted in ibid.
8. W. J. Henderson, *The Art of Singing* (New York, 1938), passim.
9. Mayer, *Grandissimo Pavarotti*, p. 31.
10. Hans Magnus Enzensberger, *Mediocrity and Delusion*, trans. Martin Chalmers (London, 1991), section titled "Twilight of the Reviewers."

11. Rolv Heuer, *Genie und Reichtum* (Gütersloh, 1971), p. 9.

12. Sloterdijk, *Critique*, p. 307.

13. Ibid., p. 308. The argument that the culture industry, especially in Germany, is subsidized, whereas the professional athlete profits from the free market, has little weight here. Both the culture industry and sports in general are intimately connected to the economic process. A professional athlete can acquire a seven-digit so-called sponsor contract if, in his or her capacity as a commercial personality, he or she can reach millions of consumers by means of the television screen, totally regardless of the fact that the broadcast stations pay these horrific honoraria from the rates their patrons pay, many of whom couldn't care less about the athlete in question. The taxpayer may be the one who pays for theater, but he is also the goose that is drawn to the box office by the industrial giants known as entertainment, leisure time, and sports.

AN IRRESISTIBLE RISE

1. Pavarotti's interviews explain in much more detail than does his book how he systematically studied the recordings of his colleagues, paying most attention to the way they handled stylistic and technical problems. This has nothing to do with the imitation of predecessors. Walter Legge reports that he trained Elisabeth Schwarzkopf into a veritable *gazza ladra*, a "thieving magpie" of singing styles.

2. This anecdote turns up in many of the histories of singing. Even Henderson repeats it in his book *The Art of Singing*.

3. Mayer, *Grandissimo Pavarotti*, p. 56.

4. Ibid., p. 58.

5. Ibid., p. 74.

6. *Opera* 8/67:692.

7. *Opera* 5/68.

8. Luciano Pavarotti, with William Weaver, *Pavarotti: My Own Story* (New York, 1981), p. 85.

9. James Joyce was an avid admirer of the tenor John O'Sullivan

and tried to praise this singer at the expense of Giacomo Lauri-
Volpi. Michael Scott quotes the absurd number of high notes—
if not the high number of absurd notes—that Joyce counted in
the second volume of *The Record of Singing*.

10. Hubert Saal, "The Great Pavarotti," *Newsweek*, March 15, 1976.

11. Richard Bonynge, "Bonynge on Bel Canto" (interview with
Stephen Wadsworth), *Opera News*, February 28, 1976.

12. Mayer, *Grandissimo Pavarotti*, p. 102.

13. Unattributed article in *Time*, September 24, 1976.

14. Sloterdijk, *Critique*. [This quotation is translated from the German original, vol. 1, p. 221.—*Trans.*]

15. This bad joke, with all its innuendo, stems from an article in the
New York Times Magazine of February 12, 1978. The author,
Stephen E. Rubin, was trying to approach in a serious and objec-
tive manner the question of why so many singers are overweight.

16. Michael Walsh, "What Price Pavarotti Inc.?" *Time*, November
30, 1981.

17. Review in the spring 1986 issue of *Opera Fanatic*, edited and
published in New York and obviously the work of a single man,
Stefan Zucker, who seems to fit all the characteristics of the title
of his journal and who bills himself as "the world's highest
tenor." A record has appeared under this title, and even after
repeated playings, I still don't know if it's a serious effort or an
involuntary parody à la *The Glory of the Human Voice* with
Frances Foster Jenkins.

18. Pavarotti has always remained loyal to Decca, his first recording
company, a rather rare occurrence in today's fast-moving world
of commercialism. Only at the very beginning of his career did
he record Mascagni's *L'Amico Fritz* for EMI. In 1989 he was
given the opportunity to sing the tenor part in Verdi's Requiem
under Riccardo Muti, but the actual performance did not prove
to be the sensation it was expected to be. The recording of the
Donizetti *buffa* with James Levine came out in 1990. Levine,
like Kathleen Battle, was one of the artists affiliated with
Deutsche Grammophon.

19. Will Crutchfield, "Pavarotti and Battle in Met *Elisir*," *New York Times*, April 23, 1989.

THE METASTASIS OF CHANGE

1. Horowitz, *Understanding Toscanini*, pp. 18, 20.
2. Mayer, *Grandissimo Pavarotti*, p. 133. Concerts such as these, which are no longer in vogue in Germany, are usually dismissed with an expression of contempt. Singers are supposed to be "serious," an attitude best demonstrated by singing the *Winterreise*, for example. This phenomenon has taken place in a society that has transformed the narcissistic productions of what they call "the people" into commercialized daily fare. I personally can't appreciate the reasoning behind the attitude that frowns upon a singer turning his innate artistic talent, that of singing, into the object of a concert, always supposing that we're still talking about art.
3. Mayer is not the only one to relate this anecdote; Pavarotti himself has frequently repeated it, and it is difficult to discover whether it's true or whether he tells it because it's so appropriate and plausible.
4. See Pavarotti, *Pavarotti: My Own Story*, p. 132. In the chapter titled "Managing Pavarotti," Breslin is clear and up front: if a talented artist could be turned into a star by managing and marketing alone, there would be many more stars than one could dream of. What is left out of this equation is that other qualities beyond the actual artistic ones are becoming more and more important: in Pavarotti's case it's the combination of a Falstaff and a gondolier, of an entertainer and a happy-go-lucky guy, of a clown and a Latin lover, of—how do the magazines put it?—a bigger-than-life Big P.
5. Jean-Pierre Ponnelle produced a television version of Verdi's *Rigoletto* with Pavarotti, Edita Gruberova, and Ingvar Wixell. Realizing that Pavarotti is not especially agile, he had him drawn through the throngs like a Caesar in a triumphant chariot. Although this happened in the very first scene, it's one

example among many. Every scene in which the Duke sang of his feelings featured the singer as mime—and this critic is quick to grant that Pavarotti gave a very evocative performance. In this film he acts not only with his voice but also with his lively, charming, winning theatrical skills.

6. Ernst Bloch speaks of a sound that comes from a physical source, in other words, one that is not transmitted by an instrument and certainly not by any technical equipment. Being moved by a musically controlled human voice is one of the most beautiful aspects of the sense of hearing—being able to experience its projection to the point of being overcome both physically and emotionally. Technical amplification, on the other hand, produces an inescapable physiological effect, and to the sensitive ear this is rather annoying.

7. Martin Mayer describes this in detail in the concluding chapter of his book, which is in many respects excellent. The only disturbing thing is the apologetic tone with which the author feels he has to justify what his colleagues, and in fact he himself, cannot justify: the lowering of an artist and of singing to the level of the cultural version of a church fair.

8. With this word I am appropriating one of the thoughts of Roland Barthes, namely, that the mythifications of everyday life rob the object, in this case the artist, of his history and his individuality.

9. Enzensberger, *Mediocrity*, the section titled "Twilight of the Reviewers."

LAUGH, CLOWN!

1. Quoted in Luca Fontana, "Che bella voce," *Transatlantik* (n.p., n.d.).

2. Ibid. A note of clarification is in order here: the word *coloratura* as it is used here refers not only to a running passage, but to the coloring of a phrase as well—a coloring achieved by technical means.

3. Ibid. The word *mimesis* refers to the imitative reflection of reality. This kind of "direct" representation of affect is one of the claims made by so-called realistic opera: it is actually a contradiction in terms.

4. Theodor W. Adorno, "On the Fetish Character in Music and the Regression of Listening," in *The Culture Industry: Selected Essays on Mass Culture* (London, 1991), pp. 85–92.

5. Pavarotti in conversation with the author. Martin Mayer begins his essay with the identical remark. It just goes to show that, as interviewer, one hardly has a chance anymore with the stars of our day: every question has already been asked at least once and is answered as confidently as the stars sing their cadenzas.

6. Franziska Martienßen-Lohmann, *Der Wissende Sänger: Ein Gesangslexikon in Skizzen* [The knowledgeable singer: A lexicon of song in sketches] (Zurich, 1966); see the section on the tenor.

7. Saal, "The Great Pavarotti."

8. Martienßen-Lohmann, *Der Wissende Sänger.*

9. Saal, "The Great Pavarotti."

10. Jürgen Kesting, *Die großen Sänger* [The great singers] (Düsseldorf, 1986); see the section on Anselmi.

11. Even if untrue, this invention is so ingenious that it has found its way into all the books about Caruso.

FROM MYTHIC HERO TO LOVER

1. Dominique Fernandez's *Porporino, or The Secrets of Naples* (New York, 1976) invokes the myth of Orpheus, the musician who could melt stones, to explain the effect of the castrato, an androgynous voice in which the masculine and feminine elements come together in synthesis. See pp. 293 f.

2. Glareanus, or Heinrich Glarean (1488-1563), was a music theorist, geographer, humanist, and poet. His *Dodecachordon*, which had an enormous influence on the music of the Renaissance, is a mixture of musical anthology, textbook, and biography—a veritable universe in itself. Falsetto (from *falso*, false) is a frequently discussed and equally frequently disputed concept,

especially since a falsetto tone is all too easily confused with a high head voice by those listeners not versed in sophisticated vocal distinctions. The latter can be heard in Figaro's aria in Rossini's *Il Barbiere di Siviglia* and particularly by its German interpreters, who, at the repetition of "Figaro, Figaro," cadence up to the high C. The effect is usually greeted with laughter, but, since even this kind of emotional reaction has its tone, it's clear that it's an embarrassed laugh occasioned by an effeminate effect. As Franziska Martienßen-Lohmann explains, the genuine falsetto is one of the head voice functions of the tenor voice primarily used in *piano* singing. The recordings of Fernando de Lucia and Mattia Battistini give a clear impression, clearer than any technical or theoretical description could ever provide, of a falsetto perfectly integrated into the dynamics of singing, especially when the singers steer toward their goal of high ornamental notes in long legato passages and show their flexibility in carefully differentiating the dynamic gradations between *piano* and *pianissimo*. They do this without giving the impression that a diminuendo necessarily means a loss of sound or even, as is often the case with Pavarotti, a reduction to a dull, muffled, incorporeal, and passive tone.

3. Henry Pleasants, *The Great Singers*, 2d ed. (New York, 1981). This book is invaluable. In it the author, himself a singer, blends the testimonies of three centuries of eyewitness reports into a panorama of singing at a time when there was not yet any acoustic documentation. One wonders whether this is why the writers—Stendhal, Musset, Heine, Burney, Chorley—developed such a rich vocabulary intended to enable the reader to actually hear what he was reading.

4. In modern revivals, these roles are usually sung in falsetto by countertenors. For his *Midsummer Night's Dream* (1960), Benjamin Britten entrusted the part of Oberon to the countertenor Alfred Deller, whose voice Sir Michael Tippett praised as the expression of purest musicality. See the section on Deller in Kesting, *Die großen Sänger*.

5. Stendhal's apotheosis of Velluti is interesting, as is his criticism of Rossini who, annoyed by his singer's mania for decoration, wrote out his parts in great detail from then on, and, in doing so, as far as I'm concerned, managed to strangle out all vocal spontaneity.

6. Emma Calvé, *My Life* (New York, 1902), pp. 63–65.

7. It is difficult to determine when the word was first used; in any case, the concept is an epitaph. It was presumably first applied to Adelina Patti.

8. Angelo Maria Amorevoli was born in Venice in 1716, sang in works by Porpora and Hasse, and was enthusiastically praised by Burney. For further information, see Stefan Zucker, "Heroes on the Rise," *Opera News*, January 4, 1986.

9. Stendhal, *Life of Rossini* (London, 1970), p. 72.

10. See Zucker, "Heroes on the Rise."

11. See Pleasants, *The Great Singers*, the section on Donzelli.

12. See Mario Praz, *Liebe, Tod und Teufel: Die schwarze Romantik* (Love, death, and the devil: Black romanticism), 3d ed. (Munich, 1988). In the introductory chapter, Praz describes an aesthetic or a sense of being "happy to be unhappy." Maria Callas provided the operatic standards; see also the introductory chapter to Jürgen Kesting, *Maria Callas*, trans. John Hunt (Boston, 1993).

13. See Carl Dahlhaus, *Nineteenth Century Music*, trans. J. Bradford Robinson (Berkeley and Los Angeles, 1989). Dahlhaus describes the essential nature of Rossini's music as "veiled."

14. Quoted in Pleasants, *The Great Singers*, pp. 132–33.

15. Ibid.

16. Ibid., p. 161.

17. Ibid., p. 162.

18. Ibid.

THE SEISMIC SHOCK

1. Stefan Zucker, "Seismic Shocker," in *Opera News*, January 1, 1983, p. 14.

2. Ibid. Zucker's article discusses in detail the development of the tenor voice between 1770 and 1840. Pleasants' book does the same.

3. See Richard Osborne, *Rossini* (London, 1986), especially the section on Armida.

4. The expression "hybrid role" is generally understood to mean a part with demands that are otherwise made only of specialists, such as both the "great tone" (*großer Ton*) and coloratura.

5. Henderson, *The Art of Singing*, p. 221.

6. Pleasants, *The Great Singers*, p. 171.

7. In his letters Verdi complained that Tamagno only sang loudly, and George Bernard Shaw spoke of "magnificent screaming." Both remarks indicate above all else that the composer as well as the critic were accustomed to a different way of producing a particular tone. Tamagno's recordings remind one of a *tenor robusto* whose singing never sounded as "broad" or as voluminous as that of Mario del Monaco. Instead, Tamagno's singing displays many lyric and sensitive phrasings, which is to say, the critical reports are also to be read against the background of contemporary taste.

8. Pleasants, *The Great Singers*, pp. 252–53.

9. Unlike Tamagno, the tenors who were and continue to be devoted to the verismo aesthetic produce a broad, full tone with the chest voice coarsely pressed into the high range. The price this exacts is the loss of color and movement, that is, the loss of all tonal beauty.

10. See Kesting, *Die großen Sänger*, "Toscanini und die Folgen" (Toscanini and beyond). It would be going too far afield in this connection to discuss the first interpreters of Richard Wagner's works. Joseph Alois Tichatschek (1807–86) was an ideal Rienzi (a fact that speaks for the quality of his *Italian* training) and a not completely convincing Tannhäuser. This latter role is probably more frequently associated with the name of Albert Niemann (1831–1917), who was also the first Siegmund. A third tenor who deserves mention here is the marvelous Ludwig

Schnorr von Carolsfeld (1836–65), whom the composer heard for the first time in 1862 in his role as Lohengrin and in whom he found his first and apparently grandiose Tristan (1862). Von Carolsfeld died at the age of twenty-nine just before a planned performance of *Don Giovanni* (as Ottavio!). Even so, we do have to draw attention to a significant incident in the history of singing. Like his Italian contemporary Verdi, Wagner paid absolutely no attention to a singer's individual talents and potentials: the idea of tailoring arias to a singer like the "well-fitting garment" that Mozart spoke of seemed ludicrous to him. The famous letter to Albert Niemann just before the Parisian performance of *Tannhäuser*, dated February 21, 1864, shows that the primacy of the singer was gradually being broken and replaced by a conception or shape of the work determined by the composer alone. Thus began the "dictatorship of the baton," which Verdi found worse than the "arbitrariness of the prima donna rondos"—an arbitrary willfulness that would eventually develop into the fetishistic concept of fidelity to the original work.

11. Ibid., the sections on Maurel and de Lucia.
12. All of the Mapleson cylinders have been overplayed by now; because of their technical quality, the recordings, copies of which can be obtained through the Metropolitan Opera, are of relevance only to the music historian. De Reszke's recordings, however, do give an impression of his style, but they say nothing about the sound of his voice.
13. Henderson, *The Art of Singing*, p. 336.

THE END OF PERFECTION

1. Henderson, *The Art of Singing*, pp. 303-4.
2. In his notes to the big EMI set, Celletti emphatically defends Gigli against the many reproaches he received by mainly Anglo-Saxon critics (see the section on Gigli in Kesting, *Die großen Sänger*). I happen to agree with those criticisms.
3. See Kesting, *Die großen Sänger*, the section on Björling. I see in

Björling an interpreter who no longer sang his parts with immediacy, but rather with a certain distanced quality; in other words, he sang from the perspective of an interpreter during opera's *post-histoire*.

4. Pavarotti has repeatedly stated that there were thirty tenors better than he when he began his career. That's coquettish and not altogether untrue—but what's also true is that he sings in a much livelier and more evocative manner than those on the list.

A NEW BEGINNING IN THE PAST

1. Fontana, "Che bella voce."
2. Valletti had a relatively brief operatic career. His recordings, however, all on the Cetra label, show what a singer with a light voice can do.
3. Evocative portrayals of this type are found less among the typical Italian tenors than among Jon Vickers (Peter Grimes, Aeneas, Tristan, Otello), Peter Pears (Gustav von Aschenbach), Nicolai Gedda (Hoffmann, Werther, Cellini, Dimitri) or Wolfgang Windgassen (Tannhäuser, Tristan).
4. Pavarotti said this in a conversation with the author.

WHAT YOU INHERITED FROM YOUR FATHERS

1. Wilfrid Mellers, *Music and Society* (London, 1946).
2. Kolodin's chronicle repeatedly points out that lyric tenors at the Met tried to compete with the *spintos* and sang themselves out in the process.
3. As examples we might mention his recitals of Russian arias, and especially Susanin's aria from Glinka's *A Life for the Tsar*. Gedda uses the *voix mixte* in almost all his recordings of the French repertoire.
4. See Martienßen-Lohmann, *Der Wissende Sänger*, the section on coloratura.
5. The *aria d'urlo* is the "air with the scream." In his later operas Mascagni called for a voice "that screams, screams, screams." He was evidently successful—in destroying voices.

6. A long essay could be written about these meaningless and stereotypical phrases, an overdue exposé of the prejudices and ignorance of critics who lay into singers for that which represents the best of their talents.

THE GREAT TRADITION

1. This criticism was advanced not only by Theodor W. Adorno, in *Die Meisterschaft des Maestro* [The mastery of the maestro] and in various other short articles, but also by critics such as Virgil Thomson and modern American composers. The young American critic Joseph Horowitz has summarized the effect of the technocratic ideal musician and of the star's direction of the musical scene in his book *Understanding Toscanini*. The consequences of a mechanically regular rather than of a rhythmically varied (rubato) musical performance on the art of singing are considerable. The "mechanization" of the tempo relegated the art of singing to a dependency on the "chronos of real time" (Igor Stravinsky). This musical development, which is present whenever sound and speed are combined, reached its peak with the invention of the gramophone record, that time machine whose inner law is probably also determined by the chronos of real time. In other words, *tempo rubato* has a different effect on a recording than it does in the concert hall, the site of experiential time.

2. "Orchesterschläge von zermalmender Wucht" [Orchestral strokes of crushing impact] is the title of an article by Gerhard R. Koch reviewing a concert the Chicago Symphony Orchestra gave during a 1970 tour. It appeared in the *Frankfurter Allgemeine Zeitung*.

3. The word *virtuosity* originally meant the virtue of competence. That this term is used today in a pejorative sense is understandable on the one hand from the point of view of a critique of mediocre bourgeois virtues; on the other hand, what rings through is the envy of those for whom the prize is far beyond their reach.

4. See the fifteen brief chapters called "The Art of the Singer" in William James Henderson's invaluable book *The Art of Singing*. Will Crutchfield expressed the same thoughts in the form of a case study focusing on the recordings of Fernando de Lucia and Mattia Battistini; see "Twin Glories: Fernando de Lucia and Mattia Battistini," *Opera News*, December 1987 and February 1988.

5. Crutchfield, "Twin Glories," p. 110.

6. Ibid. Crutchfield refers to both Alceo Galliera's and Claudio Abbado's recordings of Rossini's *Barbiere*, and if one compares them against each other, it turns out that the former is more theatrical and betrays a livelier characterization than does the latter. Only Maria Callas, however, possesses the technical superiority and vocal freedom that goes along with it to portray a character with any degree of depth. Claudio Abbado's recording has a perfect orchestral effect, but it's a functional perfection. The particle accelerator of the Rossini crescendo is set in motion in the finale, but it adds up to nothing more than mere mechanics. The singers on this recording are harnessed to the procrustean bed of the metronome, and the performances (with the exception of Teresa Berganza's) lack all vitality. This is because Messrs. Prey and Montarsolo, leading the attack with vocal gestures, strive for an expression that can derive only from the nuances of a superior vocalistic virtuosity.

7. The problem can perhaps be more easily appreciated from a historical perspective. In the 1950s Maria Callas was responsible for a strong revival of the romantic repertoire (Nietzsche would have called it a monumental history). Joan Sutherland, on the other hand, was pursuing something rather like an antiquarian approach and was restoring the old formalities of singing. She was followed by Horne, Caballé, Sills, and, in the 1980s, by an army of young interpreters, both male and female. If the reviews clearly denigrated these attempts, saying that they "had strongly committed themselves to the florid style," we are completely justified in asking in return, "To what else should these singers

have committed themselves?" Ornamentation is as integral to the vocal parts in Handel and Rossini as are the pyrotechnics to the works of Paganini or the arabesques in Chopin's nocturnes.

8. Celletti, *A History of Bel Canto*, p. 208.
9. Pavarotti, *Pavarotti: My Own Story*, pp. 67–68.
10. Mayer, *Grandissimo Pavarotti*, pp. 70, 74.
11. With this type of breathing, as anyone can easily test for himself, the stomach has to be pushed out, as it were. Nowadays, as Martin Mayer writes in his book about Pavarotti, modern women are no more permitted to have rounded bodies than Victorian ladies were permitted to have legs. In a word, the modern ideal of beauty precludes the proper way of breathing as far as singing technique is concerned. Joan Sutherland paid absolutely no attention to such conventions—her singing was more important to her than the waist was to Marie Taglioni, or to Maria Callas, who fasted to acquire her slim figure.
12. Of course, this is a highly subjective view. Pavarotti's statement does reveal an objective truth about the aesthetic corruption of the opera industry, though, which has no correctives left, least of all from the side of the critics. How long has it been since a William James Henderson wrote, "A very few singers of the type of Melba have caused more mischief in one year than two or three Sembrichs and Lehmanns could ever have done in six"? Who, Henderson asked, is responsible for the public's lack of discrimination? It certainly wasn't the public that demanded Caruso portray Canio the way he did; it wasn't the public that expected of Lotte Lehmann or Elisabeth Schwarzkopf such a sublime portrayal of the Marschallin; not the public who hoped to receive from Maria Callas the dramatic revival of Norma or the stylistic differentiation of the early Verdi roles (Leonora). The artist determines the audience's taste. Today, however, it's precisely those people in artistically responsible positions— theater managers, agents, and directors—who defend the transformation of the music scene into a type of amusement enterprise.

PAVAROTTI ON RECORD

1. John Steane, *The Grand Tradition: Seventy Years of Singing on Record* (London, 1974), p. 458.

THE KING OF HIGH C'S

1. Alan Blyth, ed., *Opera on Record*, vol. 3 (London, 1984), the section on Verdi's Requiem.
2. Helena Matheopoulos, *Divo* (New York, 1986). In the interviews José Carreras, for one example, or Plácido Domingo, for another, confess to a singing technique they themselves hardly ever apply.

MOZART AND MATTERS OF STYLE

1. Henderson, *The Art of Singing*, pp. 130, 131.
2. Sir Francesco Paolo Tosti (1846–1916) worked for a time as singing master at the English court. His cantabile style showed him to be committed to the old school, and he composed his songs primarily for the Victorian drawing room.
3. Volker Wacker in the *Neue Zeitschrift für Musik*, September 1989.
4. Susanna Benda, "Die Wogen des Meeres" (The waves of the sea), *Hannoversche Allgemeine*, n.d.
5. *Opernwelt*, December 1988. In this review idiomatic clichés stand in for thoughtfulness and expertise. The reference to *italianità* is vague enough, but is most probably meant to refer to the expressive gesture of verismo and surely not to that which Mozart's singers "introduced." During Mozart's time all singers were trained in the Italian school, be they located in London, Munich, Vienna, or Saint Petersburg. What existed was surely not *italianità*, but only the richly developed formal language of ornate and florid singing. The reference to the singing personality is also nothing more than a shortcut that seeks to sidestep a description of technical execution. "Fuor del mar" is sung not with personality but with technique.

PAVAROTTI AND ROSSINI

1. Zucker also quotes Stendhal ("Heroes on the Rise," p. 36).
2. Alan Blyth, ed., *Opera on Record*, vol. 3 (London, 1984), p. 44.
3. A distinction between the beautiful and the good voice was made early in the history of opera, and this polarization was also at the base of the controversy between Callas and Tebaldi. There are probably few listeners who would not prefer Pavarotti's voice over that of Gedda's as far as the sound is concerned, and there are probably hardly any aficionados who wouldn't acknowledge the versatility and stylistic supremacy of the Swede. All of this could lead to the apparent paradox that one can sing more beautifully with a "poorer" voice than with a so-called beautiful one.
4. See the Martinelli recording on the Preiser label.

PAVAROTTI AND BELLINI

1. *HiFi Stereophonie*, April 1981.
2. Blyth, *Opera on Record*, 2:124.
3. Ibid., 1:168.

PAVAROTTI AND DONIZETTI

1. The verb "to color" refers not only to various shadings of the voice but also to the melodic line produced by means of coloratura.
2. Celletti, *A History of Bel Canto*, pp. 193–94.
3. Blyth, *Opera on Record*, 1:175.
4. Kesting, *Maria Callas*, p 35.
5. In this early session Caruso was able to record the aria on two sides of the disc; in other words, he was not forced, as so often happens, to make do with a playing time of approximately three minutes. The opportunity to choose an extremely slow tempo for the *larghetto* enabled him to dwell long and effectively on the individual phrases, as well as to introduce *messa di voce* effects. Moreover, and completely in keeping with the *buffa* character, it

let him present the grace notes on "suoi," "che piè cercando io vo," and later, in the second verse, on "cor," as gestures. Never again has anyone heard the cry "cielo" sung with such energetic projection coupled with an absolutely controlled voice, never again the interplay of ritardando and diminuendo produced with greater effect ("si può morir"), nor the subtle coloratura run to the A with more buoyancy. This recording, considered by many of Caruso's admirers as one of his best, if not his very best, is stylistically outdistanced by Wolf Rosenberg's rendition with its free rubato, and is occasionally also critized as being a masterful anachronism. Thus it lost some of its prestige to the second lineal descendant, recorded in 1911. This is understandable from the perspective of a Toscanini-based Verdi aesthetic, but only as regards that particular rigor responsible for plunging singing into the crisis that Rosenberg was the first in this country to deplore so bitterly.

PAVAROTTI AND VERDI

1. *The Gramophone*, July 1986.
2. The Muti recording clearly shows what happens when singers are muzzled, as it were. The event—but not the drama—takes place in the orchestra, and the opera stage is peopled with marionettes.

PAVAROTTI AND PUCCINI

1. This is the argument that Ulrich Schreiber makes in *HiFi Stereofonie* and in his *Klassikführer* (Karlsruhe, 1979). Schreiber says quite correctly that the sensual appeal of this recording is so foregrounded as to give the music a "disreputable" tinge.
2. This reproach was made by other critics as well, including Osborne, Kenneth Furie, Harris, and Crutchfield.

PAVAROTTI AND HIS VERISTIC ROLES

1. See Henderson, *The Art of Singing*, the section on Melba. In the Melba Edition of EMI, Michael Aspinall analyzes the numer-

ous recordings of her singing with this precise point in mind
("The Ideal Voice of Song").

2. *High Fidelity*, June 1979.
3. Blyth, *Opera on Record*, 3:197.
4. Ibid., p. 234.
5. *High Fidelity*, 1984.

BIBLIOGRAPHY

BOOKS AND GENERAL LITERATURE

Barthes, Roland. *Mythologies.* Editions du Seuil. Paris, 1957.

Berlioz, Hector. *Evenings with the Orchestra.* Chicago, 1956.

Bloch, Ernst. *Essays on the Philosophy of Music.* Translated by Peter Palmer with an introduction by David Drew. Cambridge, 1985.

Blyth, Alan, ed. *Opera on Record.* 3 vols. London, 1979, 1983, 1984.

Budden, Julian. *The Operas of Verdi.* 3 vols. London, 1973, 1979, 1981.

Burney, Charles. *Musical Tours in Europe.* London, 1973.

Calvé, Emma. *My Life.* New York, 1902.

Celletti, Rodolfo. *A History of Bel Canto.* Translated by Frederick Fuller. Oxford, 1991.

Csampai, Attila, ed. *Idomeneo.* Reihe rororo-Opernbücher. Hamburg, 1989.

Dahlhaus, Carl. *Nineteenth-Century Music.* Translated by J. Bradford Robinson. Berkeley and Los Angeles, 1989.

Enzensberger, Hans Magnus. *Mediocrity and Delusion.* Translated by Martin Chalmers. London, 1991.

Fernandez, Dominique. *Porporino, or the Secrets of Naples.* Translated by Eileen Finletter. New York, 1976.

Henderson, William James. *The Art of Singing.* New York, 1938.

Heuer, Rolv. *Genie und Reichtum.* Gütersloh, Germany, 1971.

Horowitz, Joseph. *Understanding Toscanini.* New York, 1987.

Kesting, Jürgen. *Die großen Sänger.* Düsseldorf, 1986.

———. *Maria Callas.* Translated by John Hunt. Boston, 1993.

Kolodin, Irving. *The Story of the Metropolitan Opera.* New York, 1966.

Martienßen-Lohmann, F. *Der wissende Sänger: Ein Gesangslexikon in Skizzen.* Zurich, 1966.

Matheopoulos, Helena. *Divo.* New York, 1986.

Mayer, Martin. *Grandissimo Pavarotti: A Celebration of the Career of the World's Greatest Tenor on the Silver Anniversary of His Debut.* New York, 1986.

Osborne, Richard. *Rossini.* London, 1986.

Pavarotti, Luciano, with William Wright. *Pavarotti: My Own Story*. New York, 1981.

Pleasants, Henry. *The Great Singers*. 2d ed. New York, 1981.

Praz, Mario. *La carne, la morte e il diavolo nella letteratura, romantica*. Milan, 1930. (German translation: *Liebe, Tod und Teufel: Die schwarze Romantik*. dtv. 4375. Munich, 1988.)

Rushmore, Robert. *The Singing Voice*. New York, 1971.

Scott, Michael. *The Great Caruso*. New York, 1988.

Sloterdijk, Peter. *Critique of Cynical Reason*. Translated by Michael Eldred. Minneapolis, 1987.

Steane, John. *The Grand Tradition: Seventy Years of Singing on Record*. London, 1974.

Stendhal. *Life of Rossini*. London, 1970.

Umbach, Klaus. *Geldscheinsonate: Das Millionenspiel mit der Klassik*. Frankfurt am Main, 1990.

ESSAYS AND ARTICLES

Adorno, Theodor W. "On the Fetish Character in Music and the Regression of Listening." In *The Culture Industry: Selected Essays on Mass Culture*, 85–92. London, 1991.

Bonynge, Richard. "Bonynge on Bel Canto." Interview with Stephen Wadsworth. *Opera News*, February 28, 1976.

Crutchfield, Will. "Authenticity in Verdi: The Recorded Legacy." *Opera*, August 1985.

———. "Pavarotti and Battle in Met *Elisir*." *New York Times*, March 23, 1989.

———. "Twin Glories: Fernando de Lucia and Mattiata Battistini." *Opera News*, December 1987, February 1988.

Faria, Carlo. "A Cry of the Spirit: Bellini's Bel Canto in *I Puritani*." *Opera News*, February 28, 1976.

Fontana, Luca. "Che bella voce." *Transatlantik* (n.d., n.p.).

Hiller, Carl H. "Der Tenor in der italienischen Oper." *Opernwelt*, April 1982.

Jacobson, Robert. "Preferibilente Luciano." *Opera News*, October 1976.

Kesting, Jürgen. "Tenore di grazia." *Opernwelt*, May 1972.

Koch, Gerhard R. "Der kolossale Tenor." *Frankfurter Allgemeine Zeitung*, February 5, 1985.

"Opera's Golden Tenor." *Time*, September 24, 1979.

Osborne, Conrad L. "Diary of a CavPag Madman." *High Fidelity*, June 1979.

Saal, Hubert. "The Great Pavarotti." *Newsweek*, March 15, 1976.

Walsh, Michael. "What Price Pavarotti Inc.?" *Time*, November 30, 1981.

Zucker, Stefan. "Heroes on the Rise." *Opera News*, January 4, 1986.

———. "Seismic Shocker." *Opera News*, January 1, 1983.

INDEX OF NAMES AND WORKS